instant manager
taking control of work and life

chartered
management
institute

inspiring leaders

neuro linguistic
PROGRAMMING

MO SHAPIRO

D1102596

Hodder Arnold

A MEMBER OF THE HODDER HEADLINE GROUP

The publisher has used its best endeavours to ensure that the URLs for external websites referred to in this book are correct and active at the time of going to press. However, the publisher and the author have no responsibility for the websites and can make no guarantee that a site will remain live or that the content will remain relevant, decent or appropriate.

Orders: Please contact Bookpoint Ltd, 130 Milton Park, Abingdon, Oxon OX14 4SB. Telephone: (44) 01235 827720, Fax: (44) 01235 400454. Lines are open from 9.00 to 5.00, Monday to Saturday, with a 24-hour message answering service. You can also order through our website www.hoddereducation.co.uk.

British Library Cataloguing in Publication Data
A catalogue record for this title is available from the British Library.

ISBN-13: 978 0340 945 704

First published in UK 2007 by Hodder Education, 338 Euston Road, London, NW1 3BH in association with the Chartered Management Institute.

Typeset by Transet Limited, Coventry, England.
Printed in Great Britain for Hodder Education, a division of Hodder Headline, an Hachette Livre UK Company, 338 Euston Road, London NW1 3BH by Cox & Wyman Ltd, Reading, Berkshire.

Hodder Headline's policy is to use papers that are natural, renewable and recyclable products and made from wood grown in sustainable forests. The logging and manufacturing processes are expected to conform to the environmental regulations of the country of origin.

Impression number   10 9 8 7 6 5 4 3 2
Year   2012 2011 2010 2009 2008 2007

The Chartered
Management Institute

chartered
management
institute
inspiring leaders

The Chartered Management Institute is the only chartered professional body that is dedicated to management and leadership. We are committed to raising the performance of business by championing management.

We represent 71,000 individual managers and have 450 corporate members. Within the Institute there are also a number of distinct specialisms, including the Institute of Management Consultancy and Women in Management Network.

We exist to help managers tackle the management challenges they face on a daily basis by raising the standard of management in the UK. We are here to help individuals become better managers and companies develop better managers.

We do this through a wide range of products and services, from practical management checklists to tailored training and qualifications. We produce research on the latest 'hot' management issues, provide a vast array of useful information through our online management information centre, as well as offering consultancy services and career information.

You can access these resources 'off the shelf' or we can provide solutions just for you. Our range of products and services are designed to ensure companies and managers develop their potential and excel. Whether you are at the start of your career or a proven performer in the boardroom, we have something for you.

We engage policy makers and opinion formers and, as the leading authority on management, we're regularly consulted on a range of management issues. Through our in-depth research and regular policy surveys of members, we have a deep understanding of the latest management trends.

For more information visit our website **www.managers.org.uk** or call us on **01536 207307**.

Chartered Manager

Transform the way you work

The Chartered Management Institute's Chartered Manager award is the ultimate accolade for practising professional managers. Designed to transform the way you think about your work and how you add value to your organisation, as it is based on demonstrating measurable impact.

This unique award proves your ability to make a real difference in the workplace.

Chartered Manager focuses on the six vital business skills of:

- Leading people
- Managing change
- Meeting customer needs
- Managing information and knowledge
- Managing activities and resources
- Managing yourself

Transform your organisation

There is a clear and well-established link between good management and improved organisational performance. Recognising this, the Chartered Manager scheme requires individuals to demonstrate how they are applying their leadership and change management skills to make significant impact within their organisation.

Transform your career

Whatever career stage a manager is at Chartered Manager will set them apart. Chartered Manager has proven to be a stimulus to career progression, either via recognition by their current employer or through the motivation to move on to more challenging roles with new employers.

But don't take just our word for it ...
Chartered Manager has transformed the careers and organisations of managers in all sectors.

'Being a Chartered Manager was one of the main contributing factors which led to my recent promotion.'
Lloyd Ross, Programme Delivery Manager, British Nuclear Fuels

• *'I am quite sure that a part of the reason for my success in achieving my appointment was due to my Chartered Manager award which provided excellent, independent evidence that I was a high quality manager.'*
Donaree Marshall, Head of Programme Management Office, Water Service, Belfast

• *'The whole process has been very positive, giving me confidence in my strengths as a manager but also helping me to identify the areas of my skills that I want to develop. I am delighted and proud to have the accolade of Chartered Manager.'*
Allen Hudson, School Support Services Manager, Dudley Metropolitan County Council

• *'As we are in a time of profound change, I believe that I have, as a result of my change management skills been able to provide leadership to my staff. Indeed, I took over three teams and carefully built an integrated team, which is beginning to perform really well. I believe that the process I went through to gain Chartered Manager status assisted me in achieving this and consequently was of considerable benefit to my organisation.'*
George Smart, SPO and D/Head of Resettlement, HM Prison Swaleside

To find out more or to request further information please visit our website **www.managers.org.uk/cmgr** or call us on **01536 207429**.

Contents

CHAPTER 03

CHAPTER 04

CHAPTER 05

CHAPTER 06

CHAPTER 07

CHAPTER 08

CHAPTER 09

CHAPTER 10

HOW CAN I REDUCE MY OWN AND MY STAFF'S STRESS AND INCREASE PRODUCTIVITY?

Preface

Instant Manager: Neuro Linguistic Programming is intended to act as a resourceful companion to you in your role as a manager and leader. The tools, techniques and theories of NLP will broaden the scope of your management and enhance your management practice. NLP stems from what people do naturally, identifies what they are doing and how they are doing it so that they have increased choices in their lives. You will have more options in dealing with your staff when you can better understand how you all process information and use this to enhance your communications.

I wanted to make *Instant Manager: Neuro Linguistic Programming* as accessible and current as I could. I asked many people for ideas and case studies that would bring the theories to life. I was delighted by their responses and their generosity in taking time out of their busy schedules to fit in with mine.

Acknowledgements

I am grateful to John Overdurf and Julie Silverthorn at Neuro-Energetics together with 4Rapport Graphics for their kind permission to reproduce their *NLP Practitioner Field Manual & Study Guide* diagrams of the conscious / unconscious minds, rapport, eye accessing movements and reframing. Susan Quilliam for her kind permission to adapt the metaprogram illustration in chapter six from her book *What Makes People Tick? The Ultimate Guide to Personality Types*. Paul Z. Jackson and Mark McKergow for their kind permission to reproduce an extract from *The solutions Focus: Making Coaching and Change SIMPLE*.

Thanks especially to Francesca Giulia Mereu, Tracy Plaice, Maria Deacon-Viney, Adam Cox, Mark Jenkins, and Jenny Hinds for being my critical and enthusiastic readers. Simon Hazeldine, Andrew Whittaker, Alison Smith, Shay McConnon, Chris Davidson and Fergus McClelland for their time and case studies. John Overdurf and Julie Silverthorn for being such tranceformational teachers and permitting me to share their illustrations of NLP processes. Susan Quilliam for being my NLP sounding board. Rita Shapiro, a telephone motivator. Support, laughs and encouragement from Stephanie Holland, David Morton, David Lawson, Marie Mosely, Alison Straw and Kevin Watson. Elizabeth Haylett at the Society of Authors who helped with matters contractual. Jonathan Doyle a most flexible editor and Alison Frecknall, publisher, Hodder Education whose enthusiastic persuasion set me writing again.

Biggest thanks of all go to Mark Yoxon who has been a constant source of encouragement and support. He has read copy, sourced information, offered ideas and generally kept me in good order.

You are all stars, thank you.

Mo Shapiro

What is Neuro Linguistic Programming – NLP?

I love the idea of this book being written around a series of questions because, for me, that embodies the spirit of NLP. Questions suggest curiosity, a state of wanting to understand and engage with a phenomenon – whatever it might be. From the minute they can speak, young children ask the question 'why?'; for them, everything has to have an explanation and a reason. As we grow older we can lose that need to know and become resigned to our lot, thinking this is as good as it gets. When we reintroduce curiosity and an enquiring mind, we open pathways to a whole suite of choices and possible changes. One of my favourite NLP books is called *Using your brain for a CHANGE* because that is precisely what the tools and techniques of NLP enable you to do.

Keep tapping into your curiosity and remain inquisitive as, throughout the book, I offer you opportunities to increase your options in the way you manage yourself and your staff. You won't be surprised to know that the more you understand about yourself, the better you can be open to learning about your staff and colleagues. Communication, leadership and management are fine when you feel confident. By increasing your confidence and repeating what works, you will be more effective in your job.

Which leads me into a number of explanations of what NLP is.

NLP was developed to answer the questions:

- 'How, specifically, do individuals who are outstanding consistently achieve the results that make them outstanding?'
- 'What is it that makes the difference between somebody who is merely competent at any given skill and somebody who excels at the same skill?'

The co-founders of NLP, Richard Bandler, a computer scientist, and John Grinder, a professor in linguistics, teamed up in the early 1970s. They set out to identify the patterns used by three outstanding therapists, all of whom achieved excellent results with their clients. They were Virginia Satir, a key figure in family therapy, Fritz Perls, the founder of gestalt therapy, and Milton Erickson, one of the greatest hypnotherapists. Bandler and Grinder wanted to work out what these three did, particularly, to achieve their exceptional success, in order to reproduce the skills and then extract systems and techniques that anyone could use to replicate the results. Bandler and Grinder created a model of human excellence which identified the essential thoughts, feelings, beliefs and behaviours that made these therapists so legendary. One of the most common phrases used in NLP teaching is that 'if one person can do something, anyone can learn to do it' because that one person is the model – all we have to do is work out how they do it and start to apply their methodology.

'People become really quite remarkable when they start thinking that they can do things. When they believe in themselves they have the first secret of success.' Norman Vincent Peale

Bandler found that he could help people change the way they lived their lives by modelling Satir's, Perls's and Erickson's strategies. He copied specific aspects of their behaviour and language and discovered that he could achieve similar results and facilitated the removal of habits or patterns of behaviour that were negatively affecting and influencing his clients' lives. Grinder's knowledge of linguistics helped him devise a number of processes which fitted into an accessible model to enhance effective communication, personal change and personal development. Bandler had worked out the 'hows' of success and Grinder created the 'ways' to access them.

In *Using Your Brian for a CHANGE*, Bandler describes how a couple's counsellor unwittingly increased the antagonism in their relationship. When the wife was complaining about something the husband did, she was instructed to look at her husband and tell him about it face to face because it was essential for them to have eye contact. What this did was to ensure that the wife connected those bad feelings to the sight of her husband's face and could recreate them every time she looked at him. Bandler noticed that Satir used the same process, but turned it around to much better effect. She would ask the couple to think about special times in their courting days and when they 'start glowing', was when she asked them to look at each other, as she said: 'and I want you to realise that this is the same person you fell so deeply in love with ten years ago.' The result was a positive connection between the couple and the opportunity to start relating from a position of convergence rather than continued conflict.

Question: What reactions do your staff have to you? Do they only have experiences of you talking to them when things go wrong? Or do they associate you with a fairly rounded approach – there to congratulate, cajole and coach them?

I once had a boss who was a great motivator. She would come into my office to give me feedback about how well I had handled a situation, or she would join in our lunchtime gatherings with news of what was going on elsewhere in the company, keeping us up to date. But if I was ever asked to join her in her office, I knew I was in for trouble and that office became synonymous with bad news. I'm not sure whether she ever told me anything good in that room, but if she did, I never heard it.

Another definition suggests that NLP is the study of how human beings make sense of their world, and offers a set of techniques, propositions and beliefs for understanding how and why we do what we do. It is based on the idea that mind, body and language interact to create our individual perception of what happens around us and that these perceptions, and their accompanying behaviours, can be changed. This is sometimes known as the 'art of the possible'. Developers of NLP believe that happiness and success are the result of specific patterns of thinking that can be learned by anyone.

When I am talking to people about what I do, that I write books about NLP and management, I am often met with a blank stare or a polite smile from someone trying to look interested but who has switched off at the words 'neuro' or 'linguistic'. It can certainly be a conversation killer in many situations. I am fascinated and relieved to find that once I have explained it in my own way, there is plenty of scope to continue talking. My fellow conversationalists either want to know how NLP can help them become better at what they do, improve their relationships, make them more effective communicators or a combination of all three. They are often also pleasantly surprised to find that there are certain aspects of NLP that they do already and which are working for them. My favourite way of explaining NLP is that it is where therapy and communications combine to help people get more of what they want from their lives.

Analysis of the words:

Neuro – your thinking processes, the way you use your senses of sight, hearing, feeling, taste and smell to understand what is happening around you.

Linguistic – your words, the way you use language and how it influences you and those around you.

Programming – your behaviour and the way you organise your ideas and actions which produces expected and unexpected results.

We know that the mind and body are inextricably linked – R. D. Laing said: 'change your body, change your mind, change your mind, change your body' – and I use NLP to cement that connection. My premise is that if your mind is on your side then your body will follow, and it's much more fun to have your mind working with you and for you, rather than against you. Your mind is your internal powerhouse that steers your thoughts and subsequent actions. The messages and thoughts from your mind have a significant influence on the way you feel and the actions you take. What is in your mind affects your health and well-being. *What you think is what you get.*

I was staying with a friend who was coming to the end of her PhD. She was writing up her dissertation and had a month in which to finish it. One evening we went to a gathering of her work colleagues and she was keen to introduce me to them. As we were going round, everyone was eager to know how her studies were progressing. Each time she mentioned her dissertation, her shoulders tightened, she sighed and said 'do you know, it's become a bit of a millstone'. After hearing this about five times, I couldn't let it continue. I asked her what the millstone meant to her. 'A solid weight, grey skies, an onerous task, a heavy load round my neck that makes a dull thud in my head.' No wonder it was such an unappealing task. What's more, she was repeating this negative programming every time she introduced me to a new person. She was shocked when I pointed out what she was doing and agreed to change the message. She decided to replace the millstone with an Olympic winner's medal and with rousing music that energised her. After that, when people asked her how it was going, she smiled and said 'fine'. She was much happier going to her computer with a medal in her mind, and finished the dissertation in time.

That story sums up the essence of NLP. The more we understand how we work, the more we can change what isn't effective in our lives. What's most important in all of this is that we can monitor our internal dialogue, start to recognise our success strategies and increase how often we use them.

How do you reply if someone asks you how your new management post is going? What images does it conjure up in your mind, what are you telling yourself, how do you feel and how do you behave as a result? You will have plenty of opportunities to answer these questions as you go through the rest of the book and will be offered a variety of techniques for change.

Operating principles

As Bandler, Grinder and their colleagues studied excellence, they created step-by-step programmes defining how successful people think. They analysed what these people see, what they hear, what feelings they have and how they behave. These became tools that could be applied by anyone wanting to make changes in their lives. As part of the model, Bandler and Grinder devised a set of operating principles that create 'the difference that makes the difference'. These principles are not 'real', they serve as a starting point. They provide a potent context for acting effectively and creating excellent results when it comes to communication and change. They are an extremely useful and practical set of principles that provide a platform for personal and professional growth. When you first go through them, some may seem untenable, even awkward. Others will already be part of the way you interact and communicate with others. I have picked seven that are most relevant to this book. As you read the following principles, imagine what might happen if you accepted them? What would it be like if you presupposed these principles to be true?

The map is not the territory – every person is unique

The statement 'The map is not the territory' is attributed to Korzybski, who created the field of general semantics. Korzybski's point was this: people don't respond directly to reality, but rather to the 'maps' or 'models' of reality they have created (based on information received via the senses and combined with stored information previously received), and that exist in their nervous systems.

My way of looking at things is unique to me, yours unique to you. If you had chosen to write this book you may have studied all the same research material and the end result would have been different. That is why there are so many reference books available on any given subject. None offers complete coverage and all tend to address the key issues through their own understanding. If I accept that the different views are valid and significant, I can enlarge my map and I will enhance my communications and understand others better.

Think of the people with whom you are in contact at work, internally – colleagues, staff, senior managers – and externally – customers and suppliers. How might their maps differ from yours? If you are able to put all the different perceptions together, you will come much closer to a complete picture than if you each stay within the boundaries of your own view. If you accept this NLP principle, then you respect and rejoice in difference.

A manager who insists there is only one way (their way) to do something will have much narrower and fewer options than the manager who understands, considers and elicits the variety of 'maps' from others.

We all have all the resources we need

At various points in our life we have achieved success. The findings of NLP suggest that, if we recall the ways we did so, then we can transfer these to any present-day challenges. Erickson believed that that the unconscious mind is a storehouse of resources, memories and experiential learnings, as well as the seat of our emotions. Everything that we have ever done is stored and could be made available if we knew how to access it. Think back to when you were first appointed as a manager. After the initial euphoria, did you wonder what you had let yourself in for? Once you remember how you successfully managed changes in the past, you can bring that knowledge into your present and draw on the resources and experiences that you already have. You can continue with confidence and anticipate further successes. Whether you want confidence, energy, strength or any other personal resource, be assured that you have experienced it in the past and it is accessible to you somewhere. If you've done it before, you can do it again.

I was working with Jack, who complained about not having enough positive energy at work. He wanted to feel calmer in meetings with a particular team member but was always getting himself wound up. We discussed times when he had felt calm in other situations. This is what he emailed me after a particular meeting: 'I found my inspiring music for the journey to work and listened to Nigel Kennedy playing the Four Seasons. Curiously, it runs for exactly the same time as the trip. It helped me during the day yesterday, I felt positive and had a very positive outcome from what could have been a tricky meeting. I thoroughly enjoyed the day and once again many thanks.'

We come to work to do our best

It may not always seem to be the case, but it would be against human nature if we set out deliberately to be miserable and have a horrible time at work. It is in everybody's interest that their work is as enjoyable and fulfilling as possible. Most people do the best they can, given the system they are in. If you or your business can create the conditions for individuals to take responsibility and feel valued in their role, they will put their best into their job. If someone comes to work seemingly intent on sabotage, it may be that their needs are not being considered or that their beliefs and values are contrary to those of the company. If you were to act as if you believed, this principle would change the way you behave with someone you think is trying to cause you trouble. We will consider in Chapter 6 what their motivation might be and how you would feel if you were in their shoes.

There are a number of answers to every question

This is the belief of flexibility and creativity. If you close your mind to allow only your personal beliefs to be true then you close off many opportunities. If you are working as part of a team and are prepared to listen to all the ideas available, then a more satisfactory outcome is likely to be found. Notice whether there are certain times or people whose ideas you shut out. Is it particular people; subject areas; times; places? Now imagine that these are useful ideas and that you want to incorporate them. This can open a new way of behaving, thinking and believing.

Our decisions are best at the time we make them

If this is your starting point, you are likely to be calmer and more understanding when you are reviewing performance with your staff. You do not have to accept their decision, just that it was right for them with the knowledge they had at the time. In fact if you don't accept their decision, then take time to assess whether you have different or additional information that could help them reach another conclusion. There may even be a chance that, in the light of the ensuing discussion, you reconsider your position. If their decision has resulted in an error, remember to think in terms of feedback and learning. Staff who are frightened of the repercussions of mistakes often end up frightened of doing anything innovative.

The meaning of communication is the effect it has

What happens when you talk or write to someone and the reply you receive is completely unexpected? Sometimes you will assume that they are being awkward or ignorant in not responding the way you want. As long as you put the onus on them somehow to achieve your interpretation of what is 'right', you cannot change things. Once you understand your own part in the equation, you can consider doing something different to put across your intended message.

Sandy wanted to get more of a response from her team; she felt they didn't take her requests seriously. I asked her to demonstrate how she let them know she meant business. Her face went red, she breathed quickly and only managed to whisper what she wanted doing and why. I was not surprised the team seemed to ignore her – they probably couldn't hear her. Sandy thought she was being clear and forceful, but realised that the effect of her message was very different. Once she was able to state her needs clearly, her success increased dramatically.

Choice is better than no choice

If you've ever felt like you're banging your head against a brick wall, you'll know it's a lot easier once you've stopped. And yet on many occasions we keep trying the same approach to a situation in the hope that this time it will come good. I often come across people who feel they don't have any choice – they are stuck in their job and have to stay there. Just recognising that this is a choice – even if it's the best of a bad lot – can help them to increase their options and reconsider how they want to experience their job. They can choose to keep things as they are or they can choose to find different ways of responding, and even pretend there are bits they enjoy. The old NLP maxims hold true here: 'If you always do what you've always done, you'll always get, what you've always got'; and 'If what you're doing isn't working, do something else, anything else'. In NLP, choice is everything and this principle is a great way to encourage new ideas and procedures.

Well formed outcomes

'If you don't make decisions about how you are going to live in years to come, then you have already made a decision – to be directed by environments instead of shaping your own destiny.'
Anthony Robbins

Did you become a manager or achieve your present position by chance and because you happened to be in the right place at the right time? Or did you become a manager because it was part of your long-term planning and a goal that you had set yourself when you started your working life? Either way, if you're in a position you want to be in congratulations! If you're not, you've come to the right place to alter the situation. Identifying and establishing well-formed outcomes is a central and first step in NLP.

You will be used to setting goals and objectives to be measured against performance at work. These are often presented as SMART goals, which means *Specific*, *Measurable*, *Achievable*, *Relevant* or *Realistic* and *Time related*. In NLP, the building blocks are slightly different and I want to take you through them step by step.

Start your goal setting process assuming that you can succeed. There are no limitations, just go for all the things you'd like to do. Follow your instincts and practise being there in advance. Before anything you want to happen can occur, 'you must desire that it happen, believe it can happen and expect it to happen' (Silva).

Step 1: Make it positive – decide what you want

Many of us are quick to recognise and think about what we don't want, but if our minds are focusing on that, we are setting ourselves up to be disappointed. If that describes you, perhaps you could take what you don't want – 'I don't want to get my management role wrong' – and ask yourself: 'what do I want instead?' The answer might be: 'to be an effective manager whose staff trust me and will grow and develop alongside me.'

Consider this. Just stop what you're doing and for the next ten seconds do not think of Donald Duck. No, don't think of Donald Duck.

Now, be honest: did you see a picture of Donald Duck? Did you hear a little quack? Did you see a beak? Did you hear any sounds or just get a sense of Donald Duck? Maybe you were awkward and you saw Mickey Mouse. The point is, I asked you *not* to think about Donald Duck and you *did*. Now why did you do that? Are you a particularly awkward person? Are you someone who always does what you're asked *not* to do? Or are you just a normal person like everyone else who, when they're told not to do something, has to think about what it is they're not going to do before they don't do it? The brain cannot recognise negatives, so when you tell yourself what not to do or not to think about, that is at the forefront of your mind and you are programming yourself to do just that. More importantly, you are also stopping yourself from concentrating on what you do want. A colleague of mine went into a meeting with Age Concern volunteers, telling himself: 'I mustn't call them "Help the Aged".' Needless to say, he was horrified when his opening words were: 'I want to acknowledge the wonderful work achieved by the volunteers here at "Help the …"' How much better he would have fared if he had told himself to be sure he spoke about the 'Age Concern' volunteers.

What do you want to achieve from reading this book? What do you want to be able to do by the end of it?

Step 2: Be specific – what exactly do you want?

It is really important to describe your goal in as much detail as possible, both for your conscious and your unconscious mind. This way, you are reinforcing the direction you want to take and giving yourself as much help as possible to get there. The best way is to ask the following questions: *when*, *where* and with *whom* do you want to achieve this outcome?

When?

Set yourself a time which might be to meet a particular deadline or over a series of time slots. Do you want read this book in readiness for your next presentation to the team or perhaps to have digested the chapter on appraisals before the round of performance reviews? Do you want to include ideas from it in various forthcoming team briefings?

Where?

In some cases you may have a specific location in mind for your objectives, in others it may take place throughout the business. Perhaps there is one site that is more challenging than the others or one particular area that needs to be reorganised. One of the objectives to arise from a team-building session I ran recently was that the open plan office needed changing – it was not conducive to harmonious working. Staff felt that they were partitioned off to such an extent that sub-teams were forming and they were not communicating as effectively as they would like. Until the session, many of them felt it was 'just me' and kept quiet. Once it was out in the open, they were keen to go back and try a number of combinations until they felt comfortable and more connected.

With whom?

Are there any key people who will be involved in this outcome? Do you need input or support from members of your team or management to help your success? You might want to help a staff member to be more confident in their approach to customers and will achieve this with some of the techniques like *anchoring* (Chapter 5) and *bell jar* (Chapter 10) which are described later in the book.

Step 3: Evidence – how will you know that you've achieved it?

What needs to be happening around you for you to know that you have got what you want? You need some way of measuring what you are doing. The best way is to collect feedback, both internally from yourself and externally from those around you. If you decide how your success will look, feel and sound, and you focus on it, you will create a greater chance of it happening. Imagining you have achieved the outcome already is another way of having your mind work with you, starting the experience in advance. Think back now to previous accomplishments and how they have affected you. You will start to recognise what pictures you saw, what you said to yourself or heard others say to you, and what emotions and sensations your success created in your mind. You might have seen a beautifully bound contract of agreement, been jumping for joy or hearing uproarious applause? Other external evidence can come in the form of positive 360 degree appraisal, satisfied customer feedback, improved sales, a pass certificate or a team meeting where everyone is smiling and relaxed.

Step 4: Fit – how will you feel when it's happened?

This question enables you to check how your stated outcome fits in with other aspects of your life and your overall ambitions. If you find yourself answering in a half-hearted way, 'I suppose it will be fine', then you have some clear information that you have not yet defined a well-formed outcome about which you can feel passionate. And if you are not thrilled and excited by your goal, you are unlikely to want to put any energy into achieving it. Put another way, if I were to ask you: 'if you could have your outcome now, would you take it?', anything other than a resounding 'Yes' would suggest going back to the original goal and refining it.

It is also important to check that the outcome fits in with your sense of who you are as a person and what matters to you. If your outcome is not aligned to your values, you will find yourself uncomfortable and confused as you try to achieve it. I worked with someone who had picked a job in market research because she wanted to continue her social psychology studies. She loved going out and doing testings and tastings, and then drawing conclusions about what mattered to the consumer. On one occasion she came up with the 'wrong' results – they didn't fit the clients' needs. She was instructed to massage the figures. She felt compromised and uncomfortable. She had to question whether this was a job she could continue.

How does the outcome fit in with other aspects of your life and your overall plan? Are there other people or factors you need to take into account? Once you enter wholeheartedly into this outcome, will others be able to live with you in a way that works? I can become completely absorbed once I have agreed to take part in a drama production and have been known to organise the rest of my life around it. That works for me because my family and friends support me and want me to succeed. It is brilliant when they come to the show and enjoy the performance.

I was helping a colleague's daughter decide what to read at university. We spent a couple of hours working through ideas, options and possibilities. We had what we thought was a well-formed outcome: to go to Glasgow University next October to study Maths. 'How's that?' I asked with relief that we had got there. 'Oh it's OK', was the response. Back to the drawing board and we ascertained that although it had been dismissed earlier, there had to be a place for music. 'How about a joint degree?', I asked tentatively. 'Could I really do that? That would be amazing. Oh wow that's what I want to do'. I rest my case.

Step 5: Ownership – is it yours?

Whose outcome is it? Be aware of whether you are dependent on someone else for your success. If you are waiting for others to change, you risk becoming a passive or even frustrated spectator. So consider your own part and contribution to the process.

Your goal needs to be crafted in a way that means you can achieve it no matter what other people do. In a sense, this step is encouraging you to be active rather than passive. If your outcome is to have a team that is continually in the top ten achievers in the business, that is not totally under your control. If it is dependent on other people doing, or not doing, certain things, you cannot be sure to attain it. 'I will take the time to understand each team member's motivations and help them reach their full potential' is something you can do and it will ensure greater success.

Step 6: Action – what's the first step?

Nothing is achieved without action. You can spend hours designing a brilliantly well-formed outcome. You can sit back and admire it and be pleased with yourself. Until you take the first step, you can't start the journey. What is the first thing you can do to make your outcome happen? Perhaps you want to talk to all the members of your team individually, especially if they are new to you. What is your key message and how much information can they manage in one session? The rest of this book is designed to help you understand how different people process information and how they like to give and receive it. This will prove invaluable when you plan any meetings and you will be able to craft them to cover all the possibilities. Decide the order in which you want to see team members so that you are all comfortable. To make it easier for yourself, you might start with the 'unproblematic' interviews before tackling anyone who might at first seem more of a challenge.

Well-formed outcomes are central to NLP techniques. You will make more significant changes if you know what you want and what it involves. Below, I have taken 'writing instant manager NLP' as a worked example of a well-formed outcome.

Make it positive	
	● I want to write a book that will help readers understand themselves and their colleagues better.
	● I want to make it fun, with stories that will make readers think and give them options to change.
	● I want to enjoy revisiting my NLP theory and remember why it works.
	● I want to be able to use the book as the basis for a new presentation and workshop.
Specifics When	● Deadline agreed with publisher.
	● Set out dates to research and dates to draft.
	● Agree times for readers to have copy.
	● Date for final copy before handover.
Where	● Reading on train journeys.
	● Writing in my office.
	● Talking about it wherever I can.
With whom	● Source colleagues with whom I can talk issues through and work out my ideas.
	● Case studies agreed with colleagues.

Evidence	<ul><li>Completed manuscript.</li><li>Desk cleared of resource material.</li><li>Hear myself talking to groups and media about my latest book.</li></ul>
Fit	<ul><li>Massive sense of achievement.</li><li>Great to be helping people grow with NLP as I have.</li><li>It's one of the things I'm here to do.</li></ul>
Ownership	<ul><li>Having experience of writing books, we all know what to expect and are prepared to do so during the agreed timetable.</li><li>I have huge support at home and my friends know that I will be less attentive and accessible.</li></ul>
Action	1. Design an outline that covers what I want to impart. 2. Agree contract and publisher revisions. 3. Start research. 4. Create folders for each chapter and accompanying notes. 5. Start writing. 6. Revise. 7. Submit final manuscript. 8. Agree/approve cover. 9. Revise with editor. 10. Await the final copy.

We know from the autobiographies of people who have succeeded in all walks of life that they dreamt about their eventual outcome regularly and sometimes from an early age. They focused on their goals almost as an obsession. They could picture themselves achieving, hear the acclaim and feel the sense of satisfaction and excitement as they succeeded. Many of them were mocked for having dreams beyond their means, but they believed in themselves and they triumphed. They would notice others who succeeded too and, where appropriate, copy their strategies for success. These are patterns that underpin the NLP steps to well-formed outcomes.

Conclusion

An exercise in modelling

Think about managers that you have experienced. Concentrate on the one(s) who were great for you, did the most to encourage you, believed in you and helped you achieve the management position you now hold. Then note down or record:

- What did they do that made them effective?
- What do you do already that is like them?
- What else do you need to do to be like them?
- If you are still in contact with them, find out how they think they do what they do. It is perfectly fine if they make up the answers – their unconscious will know.
- Take one of their behaviours or attitudes and introduce it into your management practice. Notice what happens.
- Once you are delighted with that, take another, then another, until you have incorporated all that you want.
- Notice the feedback and response.
- Enjoy the changes.

INSTANT TIP

Focus on what is working in your management routine and record your successes.

02

What makes people tick?

You know how sometimes you think there is more going on with someone than meets the eye? This chapter will help you find out what that might be, as you discover more about processing both at a conscious and an unconscious level. People create reality through their language and behaviour, both of which are informed by their beliefs and values. Many are accessed automatically and may not be questioned until there is a conflict or clash of ideas that needs to be addressed.

NLP techniques and applications are designed to help you understand what is happening at the unconscious level, where your memories, beliefs, identities and past experiences are stored. This is the place to influence change. So much of what you do is by necessity automatic. Fortunately, most of us do not have to go through a lengthy process and series of thoughts to decide how to physically get out of bed in the morning, clean our teeth or eat our breakfast. Imagine how long it would take you to do anything if that were the case. In these instances it is great to know that your unconscious mind is looking after you and your interests. Your unconscious runs the habits that make your life flow smoothly and enables you to function on an everyday basis. Unfortunately, there are some habits you have that will be counter-productive and

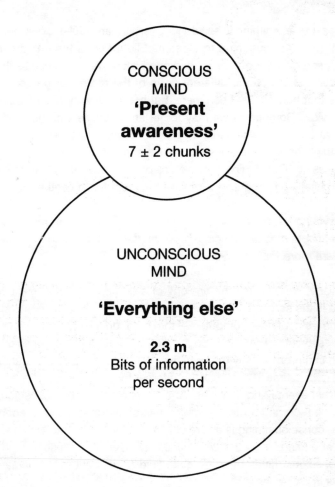

Figure 2.1: Conscious and unconscious minds.

these are ones that you can consider changing with NLP. You are an amazing learning machine. You need to learn many behaviours and habits only once before your unconscious mind puts them on auto pilot and you do not have to think again about doing them.

Your conscious mind represents your present awareness, wherever your thoughts are focused now. Your unconscious represents everything else. John Overdurf and Julie Silverthorn liken the conscious mind to a beam of light from a torch that can be directed through a large, darkened room. As you change the direction of the beam, different parts of the room can be seen – parts that had always been there, but had previously been hidden from view. Sometimes we may forget about the rest of the room, only attending to what is lit, thinking that that is all there is. When we think about who we are, we have to engage in conscious processing. Concluding that we are only who we think we are is like mistaking the lighted portion of the room for the entire room.

'Everything in the body is communicating with everything else and it's all happening unconsciously. No matter what you think you are, you are more than that.' Overdurf and Silverthorn

Similarly, we can use the analogy of a computer. The conscious mind is the screen – the pane you are looking at. The unconscious is the rest of the computer – the hard drive, database, word processor etc. There is a suggestion in NLP that the conscious brain can process only between five and nine pieces of information at any one time. These can be internal thoughts and feelings or external events and activities. At the same time, the unconscious may be receiving up to two million bits of information per second. If the conscious mind is aware only of the information to which we are attending, then the boundaries between the conscious and unconscious minds must be quite fluid to account for immediate shifts in awareness.

If the people you are working with know only that what they are doing is not the most effective way to act, they cannot change unless they find the source of their behaviour and recognise that they have choices. The influence of Milton Erickson explains why NLP focuses on the role of our conscious and unconscious processing in what we do and how we do it. These days, people are far more aware that they have an unconscious mind that stores memories and thoughts. As a manager it is vital that you can appreciate the source of your behaviour and that of your staff if you want to make changes. The trick is to find ways to access their unconscious.

The conscious mind, particularly in western cultures, always has to know *why* things happen and *why* we behave in particular ways. The more we think about *why* we do things, the more we seem to embed the unwanted behaviour into our psyches because we are keeping it at the forefront of our mind. Another 'Donald Duck' moment (see Chapter 1).

Your conscious mind is wherever you happen to be pointing it at any given time. I am sure you have been in a busy, noisy environment, like an open plan office, where there are phones ringing and many conversations occurring. You are perfectly able to focus on your phone call or the work at your computer as you fade out all the other noise that does not affect you. Then someone at the other side of the office mentions your name or the name of one of your accounts and you pick it out as if it was being spoken to you. This illustrates that, unconsciously, you are aware of many, many pieces of information every second of your life – sounds, colours, thoughts, etc – yet your conscious mind allows you to focus upon what is pertinent or relevant to you at that moment.

Your unconscious mind knows more about you than you consciously know yourself. You are currently breathing, your heart is beating (I do hope!) and your body is regulating its temperature. It is doing a range of wonderful things without you consciously having to think about it. You don't sit around thinking 'I really must remember to breathe'.

Beliefs

'To be a great champion you must believe you are the best. If you're not, pretend you are.' Muhammad Ali, heavyweight boxing champion

What exactly do we mean when we talk about 'beliefs'? In NLP terms they represent the assumptions we make about ourselves, others in the world, how we expect things to be and how we act as a result. These assumptions determine the way we behave and shape our decision-making processes. They are often based on emotions rather than facts. We tend to notice 'facts' that reinforce the beliefs. For example, if you believe 'that everyone is easy to get along with', you will only notice how well you interact with people. If, however, your belief is that 'you can't trust anyone', you will be suspicious and expect to be duped. The chances are you will give that impression too and people will be wary of you. Hence the term 'self-fulfilling prophecy' – what you believe about yourself is what happens to you. It is almost as if we attract only ideas which feed our beliefs rather than those which contradict them.

Every experience you have had and every person you have met will, in some way, have shaped your values and beliefs. We are not always consistent and may simultaneously hold values and beliefs that are contradictory. The result is that we can feel pulled in opposite directions.

A colleague of mine is very concerned about the planet and what is happening to the environment. He does all he can to keep his ecological footprint as small as possible. When he decided to celebrate a successful piece of new business, he bought disposable paper plates, cutlery and plastic cups to keep costs down. His environmental values were in conflict with his financial ones.

Have you ever encountered someone who keeps telling you that no-one can help them? No matter what you do or say, they always have a reason why it's not right for them. In the end, you probably give up and have successfully reinforced their belief that no-one can help them. They are not being deliberately obstructive, even though it may seem that way. They have held their belief for many years and would have to face many challenges in order to let it go. These beliefs are so familiar that we often do not know they are there until someone starts to ask questions like: 'who says so?'

and 'what would happen, what would it be like if someone *could* help you?'.

Begin to notice which beliefs drive your thoughts, feelings and actions. If your behaviour is not what you want and you think you can't change it, then you have probably identified a limiting belief. If your beliefs are supportive and empowering, keep them. If they are restrictive, discard them. How do you know what to believe? You don't have to dwell too much on the origin of your beliefs, but knowing who or where they came from can help you understand what they mean to you. It can sometimes help you to make changes. We are generally given injunctions with the best will in the world and for a very good reason at the time. Trace back and identify the roots of what you believe about yourself – notice where they originate. Can you hear someone telling you to have that belief? Can you picture being told, maybe more than once, or did you just sense what was expected of you? Perhaps you were told you couldn't sing, couldn't draw, would never make anything of yourself? If so, now is the chance to check whether they still hold – or were ever – true.

A coaching client of mine had reached a stumbling block in an otherwise very successful career. She kept missing out on promotion because she couldn't drive and wouldn't learn. We discovered that she had been told by her father that driving was dangerous – you're in charge of killing machine that weighs a ton. No wonder she didn't want that responsibility.

It may well be the case that you have beliefs that no longer support you – their purpose is obsolete. Sometimes we choose, or have imposed on us, beliefs that are restrictive in nature. We bring them with us into all kinds of situations. Once we recognise them, we can choose to replace them or discard them completely. If you approach the question from the other side, you may be following the belief: 'I have learnt many things in my life, now is the time to update my repertoire.' Just think about the many beliefs you have already relinquished throughout your life. Perhaps you don't believe in Father Christmas or the tooth fairy any more. And, more seriously, there will be things you have achieved that were not originally in your belief bank. I once had a boss who told me I couldn't write. It took me years and five books in print to let go of that belief.

Which of your beliefs help or hinder you? Compulsive language which includes 'should', 'ought' or 'must' leads to patterns of behaviour that can become compulsive. Check out your belief statements and ways to change them with the following questions.

Belief: 'I must never make mistakes'
Question 1. *Is this an empowering belief?* 'No'. It is the kind of belief that stops some people from trying out something new.
Question 2. *Is this a limiting belief?* A 'Yes' answer is likely here. It means you might take too long over a piece of work, just to be sure.
Question 3. *Where has it come from?* The answer here could be school, parents or any authority figures. We ask this question so you know whose belief it is.
Question 4. *What was the positive intention behind it?* This takes away any sense of blaming and enables understanding of why you were given it. The answer then may focus around wanting to encourage you to do your best, something you might not have understood at the time.
Question 5 *How do you want to change it?* Here you can substitute a new empowering belief to start telling yourself instead: 'I can make mistakes and I can learn from them.' Create one that is yours and is relevant to you.

This is a common limiting belief that can hold people back in their work. They can seem lazy, uncommitted and indecisive. If you encounter this, think about ways of checking how it might be replaced with an more useful belief. Find examples of when they have behaved quickly and successfully or give them opportunities to do so.

What exactly do you mean?

The language you use expresses the beliefs and values you hold. The very meaning of the words you use can be more complicated that they sound. You know what *you* want to say and *you* know what the words mean. The challenge arises when you are speaking in your own 'shorthand', expecting the message to be understood, or even acted upon, by someone else. It is unfortunate if, as far as the other party is concerned, you have only given out half the 'story', or one that has different interpretations. Your words do not always relay the meaning you intend because your audience will interpret them with their own representation. Just as there are national and regional dialects, so there are individual meaning dialects too. When you are asked 'fancy a drink?', do you know exactly what that means? The answer depends on the context and your familiarity with the questioner.

Award-winning speaker, Shay McConnon, opens his keynote speeches with a lovely description of what makes people tick and what leads to misunderstandings. He does this in the context of research which suggests that 75 per cent of staff leave their jobs because of relationship issues with their managers. This is a shocking thought, and a statistic that can be avoided if you take a step back to find out where your staff are coming from, rather than assuming you already know.

Shay starts with the idea that:

'... we are all wandering through life like plain tin cans with no labels. We all look the same to a lesser or greater extent. In the case of the cans, we're the same height and same dimensions, there are no distinguishing features. We make

assumptions about each other – I have feelings, you have feelings, what's inside me is what's inside you. We're just the same. I treat you as I treat myself. As I'm mushy peas inside my tin, I like to be put on a low heat and cooked gently for five minutes. You look the same so you must be mushy peas too, I'll put you on a low heat and cook you gently for five minutes. That's fine, unless inside your tin you happen to be fruit cocktail and were hoping for a couple of scoops of ice cream. By cooking you slowly on a low heat, I have just ruined you career or your life.'

Easy to do, but not so easy to remedy. If you start your interactions with 'you' as the reference point, you are setting yourself up for tension and trouble. You need to begin by finding out what's inside the other person's tin and how they want to be 'cooked' or treated. Then you can be in the 25 per cent of managers whose staff stay in the *business* because of the relationship, not *despite* it.

Meta model

For those occasions when you want to know clearly and specifically what the words mean you can use the NLP process known as the meta model.

> The meta model is used to elicit unconscious processes in language to expose the belief or value that is behind the words. It identifies ambiguities and targets them with questions.

There are times, both at work and outside, when it is crucial that we are clear and precise in what we say. If you are the health and safety officer who states that; 'there mustn't be too many people at this gathering because of the fire risk', that won't do. Equally, if you are talking in terms of a multi-million pound deal and you suggest a profit share of 'around 10 per cent-ish' or in an appraisal meeting you say 'you're always out of touch with rest of the section'. You are not providing information in a form to which others can make a valid response. This is not a case of you being deliberately awkward, just missing out some information that you assume they know. At other times it is fine to be imprecise because we are with someone who understands our shorthand or we want to encourage creativity. You can do this deliberately using the Milton model, which is described in detail in Chapter 7.

'Common sense is the collection of prejudices acquired by age 18.'
Einstein

Linguistic research suggests that there is a difference between 'deep' and 'surface' structure levels of language. *Deep structure* describes the complete and whole experience you go through unconsciously before saying the words that convey your message. *Surface structure* represents the words you speak internally to yourself (your own personal shorthand) and, audibly, to others. It is the conscious re-presentation of your deep structure. If you put all your deep structure thinking into words, the most basic narrative would take so long that you would lose your audience. Between deep structure and surface structure we *delete*, *distort* and *generalise* our experience before our thoughts are translated into words.

The meta model provides the techniques to enable you to recover information from another person which they have deleted, distorted or generalised en route from their deep structure. This avoids you wondering if you have guessed right. You can fill in the gaps and reconnect to the fuller meaning. When you are wondering 'why are you saying this?', 'what exactly are you trying to tell me?' or 'what do you want me to do?', the meta model provides a set of more elegant questions to help you find out. If we don't ask the questions, we may find we have moved a long way down conflicting paths because of an unnecessary misunderstanding. The meta model will help you and your staff to give and receive clear communications, you won't have to rely on assumptions or conjecture – you will be working from a shared understanding.

Deletions

We select only parts of the information available in deep structure and we omit much more which will inevitably lead to deletion. The following are the most common deletions.

Unspecified nouns

In this pattern you describe an action without clarifying *who* carried it out. This is sometimes used when the speaker wants to express their dissatisfaction and to avoid conflict by not naming names. It also depersonalises situations where the speaker seems to be a passive bystander – so taking no responsibility for what is happening.

He's not liked	– who specifically doesn't like him?
They don't tell you anything	– who exactly?
It's so difficult	– what precisely is so difficult?

Unspecified verbs

In this pattern you describe an action without clarifying *how* it was carried out. Most companies have mission and vision statements. These tend to describe what the company proposes to do in broad terms. The employees are expected to read between the lines or to ask pertinent questions to determine specifically how they can execute the proposals. On other occasions you may want to understand the behaviour behind a particular action, you need to know *how* something was done.

We will be the most efficient	– how exactly will we be the most efficient?
She's avoiding me	– how specifically is she avoiding you?

Nominalisation

'Any *communication* which includes lengthy *discussions* in an *organisation* is likely to lead to *confusion*!' What on earth did you take that sentence to mean? It is full of nominalisations. The word 'nominalisation' is used to describe what happens when we take a verb or process which is dynamic and change it into a noun so that it becomes static. (These are also referred to as abstract nouns.) Meta model questions enable you to find out the process or actions that are missing.

Any communication	– how do you communicate?
Lengthy discussions	– what are you discussing?
Organisation	– what are you organising?
Confusion	– how are you confusing yourself?

Nominalisations are common in business and politics. They are often deliberately vague and abstract, meaning any number of different things to different people. Nominalisations become a challenge when they are mistaken for reality and you think they actually exist. Nominalisations delete so much information that we take the empty shell and fill it with our own ideas and assumptions. Compare 'raising the stakes' with 'development in investments'. The first describes an active process, while the second is static and implies no active participation. The skill is to turn them back into active processes by establishing who is doing what and how.

Nominalisations can be recognised when the passive noun makes sense if you put the word 'ongoing' in front of it. An ongoing relationship or ongoing enterprise make sense, but an ongoing dog does not. The other test is whether or not 'it' will fit into wheelbarrow. You would struggle to put development or training into a wheelbarrow, whereas several dogs would probably fit quite comfortably.

Comparisons

Sometimes we can make a statement that implies a comparison but it is unclear what we are comparing. Our listener, rather than assuming, will want to know the rest of the information.

... resulting in greater customer loyalty	– greater compared with what?
She's better at organising	– better than whom?

Judgements

'It is a truth universally acknowledged, that a single man in possession of a good fortune, must be in want of a wife.' Jane Austen's opening sentence in *Pride and Prejudice*. If this were spoken, rather than the opening lines of a novel, you might be inclined to reply 'says who?'. Yet these kinds of global statements can be very powerful and are often received without question. The speaker is deleting the fact that this is an *opinion* and expressing their beliefs as if they were an absolute *fact*. They are presenting their map of the world as the only one. In addition, they do not identify who is making the judgement. It may be important for you to know the source of the judgement before deciding how to respond. It can also help the other person to consider 'who said this in the first instance?' and 'is it still relevant or useful for me now?'.

That is the way to do it   – according to whom?
His incompetence is worrying   – who thinks he is
                                               incompetent?

Distortions

Distortions occur when the speaker makes conclusions that have no logical foundation or assumes faulty connections between different parts of their experience. The meta model questions here elicit the evidence you have (or the other person has) to suggest that their distortion is fact.

Mind-reading

These are the kind of interpretations people make when they presume that they know what someone else is thinking or feeling. It is important to check whether this intuitive response to someone is accurate or whether it could be affecting a relationship on the basis of guesswork. The questions 'How can you be sure?' and 'How do you know?' will help you assess the meaning behind the behaviours which lead you to your conclusion.

He's ignoring me	– how do you know?
I'm sure she loves surprises	– how can you be sure?

You can also turn this mind-reading around so that you give another person the power to read your mind. They then become responsible for your well-being or otherwise and can be blamed for not understanding you. The classic 'You'd know if you really loved me' is a typical example of this. The meta model question in response would be: 'How would I know?'

Complex equivalent

This often follows mind-reading because it links two statements as if they have the same meaning – you are frowning, that means I'm in trouble. Here, frowning is equated with being in trouble, which is not necessarily the case. Some people frown when they are concentrating. The same gesture can have different meanings in different cultures. The questions for this pattern is to ask: 'How does this mean that?'

He's ignoring me	– how do you know?
He didn't wave back when I drove past him this morning. Therefore he must be ignoring me	– how does his not waving mean he is ignoring you?

Cause and effect

This pattern involves one thing having a causal relationship with another. Rather than the complex equivalent – assuming x means y – here the distortion is that x causes y and there is some sequence to the events. Use of the word 'but' is sometimes a clue to this pattern.

I was going to say something but knew it would ruin things	– how would saying something ruin things?
Involving the top team will lead to solvency	– how will involving the top team cause us to become solvent?

Presuppositions

These do exactly that and presuppose an underlying assumption about our beliefs and expectations. The classic question 'When did you stop beating your wife?' presupposes that beatings have happened and have now stopped. Whatever your answer, you are in a no-win situation. The responses to presuppositions are likely to include: 'What makes you think ...?', 'What leads you to believe ...?', or 'How do you know ...?'

When you go to the meeting, are you voting for or against? (presupposes you are going to the meeting and have decided which way to vote)	– what makes you think I am going to the meeting? How do you know I'm voting?
... you know? (a shorthand that presupposes the other person knows what we are talking about – very often we agree when we have little or no understanding)	– no, I don't know. What exactly do you mean?

Generalisations

Generalisations involve taking one experience which becomes an absolute truth in any circumstances. They also describe the rules or limits which govern our behaviour. When these are operating as part of our beliefs, we can seem to be dogmatic and rigid in discussions. Often there is an element of fear attached to the very idea of being able to change or release these strongly held views. Generalisations are divided into 'universal quantifiers' and 'modal operators'.

Universal quantifiers

The language of universal quantifiers is likely to include such words as: *always*, *every*, *never*, *no-one*, *everyone*, *all* or *nothing*. These words are all inclusive and allow no room for manoeuvre. The meta model helps the speaker to recognise that their statement is not necessarily based on reality. They can then begin to expand and change their perceptions. One response you can make is to repeat back the key words with emphasis and then exaggerate to show how inane it is.

'I'm always the last to know' – Always? – You're right of course. Everyone else in the whole business world knows before you do.' Take care how you use this or you may not get the outcome you want.

Another way of responding is to check for a counter-argument.

'Managers don't care about staff' – Has there ever been a time when a manager cared for you?'

Modal operators of necessity

These relate to the conditions and rules by which we run our lives. They implicitly seem to call on an unseen authority or unwritten rules, often originating in childhood. Modal operators of necessity are indicated by words like, *should*, *ought*, *must*, and *have to*, or their negative equivalents. These are all words which externalise responsibility. By asking the question 'what would happen if you did not do this?', you elicit the consequences of breaking the potentially constraining rule. This, in turn, enables the speaker to evaluate the present relevance of this rule.

I must be available for work	– what would happen if you weren't?
I shouldn't speak to strangers	– what would happen if you did?

Modal operators of possibility/impossibility

When a person says, 'I can't' or 'It's impossible', they are talking about something that they perceive to be outside their ability or sphere of influence. In fact, it might just be their perception which is limiting them, not their ability or their situation. If this pattern goes unchecked it can impair personal development as well as interpersonal relationships.

Whenever you find yourself saying 'can't' or 'I'll never manage that', check whether it is more a case of 'won't', 'I haven't learned yet' or 'I don't want to'. You can instantly broaden your possibilities. You might also ask yourself, 'What's stopping me?'. This will give you many insights into your map of the world.

As with the operators of necessity, you can also ask the question: 'What would happen if I did?' This is a very powerful question and can empower people to go beyond the barriers they build for themselves. It is a great way to open up someone's mind.

I can't manage	– what would happen if you could?
I should go to the meeting	– what would happen if you didn't?

The first statement suggests that the person has some notion of managing – or how else do they know they are not doing it? As they start to consider what would happen if they *could* manage, they start to imagine possibilities and shift their thinking.

Summary

Each of the specific language patterns has a legitimate and useful place in everyday communications. There are times when you might choose to be vague, allowing and encouraging others to locate their own understanding. The meta model provides an invaluable set of precision questions for those occasions when you need or desire to be absolutely clear in your own mind exactly what someone is saying to you. Begin to notice any deletions, distortions and generalisations in your own internal dialogue. You can then begin to extend your choices and your map of the world.

The meta model works because it provides and enables you to ask unexpected questions. Most people accept deletions, distortions and generalisations without question. They are more likely to inject their own meaning and carry on regardless. It is only when there is a clash that you find out how different your understanding was. The surprise element of the meta model questions is sometimes enough to jolt someone into challenging their own thinking and help you both to understand them better. ('Better than what?', I hear you ask!)

Warning. Overuse of this model can be a very effective way to lose your team or your friends. It can seem either an aggressive technique or overly pedantic. The questions are much better received if you have already established rapport. As with all NLP techniques, the aim is to be elegant and appropriate in their use. Take some time to practise the questions in your own way, until they sound natural. The ones used today are guidelines.

Conclusion

A reminder to help you familiarise yourself with meta model questions.

Notice when the information you give might not be as full as it could. Do you tend to delete, distort or generalise?

Deletions
Who, what, where, when, how specifically?
Compared with what? According to whom?
How is this being done?

Distortions
How does this mean that?
How does this cause that?
How do you know?
What leads you to believe ...?

Generalisations
Always? Never?
Has there ever been a time when ...?
What would happen if you did?
What is stopping you?

INSTANT TIP

Recognise and work to remove limiting beliefs.

03

Isn't it manipulative?

It is certainly the case that NLP gets its fair, or maybe unfair, share of bad press. People are sceptical about the claims its practitioners make and worry about its use or misuse. Many NLP books and courses include the word 'influencing', which can be confused to mean 'manipulating', at which point people want to distance themselves and go no further in discovering what it really means. This is about the root of the manipulation accusation. There is a concern that once someone is trained in NLP they will be able to sell you numerous items you don't want or persuade you to do something that is in their interest but not necessarily in yours. They don't want to become that type of person or associated with that kind of practice.

What 'influence' means in NLP is not manipulation in a bullying way. None of us likes that kind of manipulation, we feel we have been taken advantage of or tricked in some way. We may not notice it at the time, although we often feel uncomfortable about it after the event. However, we are much more likely to accept being influenced when we feel we are exercising free will in any decision or action we take. In some ways, however, all communication could be considered manipulative. It is about getting others to accept our suggestions, follow our instructions, respond to our requests or consider our ideas. Influencing people through communication is what we do anyway. So the question has to be:

'Would you like to be able to do it better, understand what you are doing and have a greater choice in your behaviour?' If you recognise that you are influencing someone unfairly, you can choose to back off and give them space to make up their own mind. You can adjust your side of the discussion in such a way that it becomes more appropriate. If it is not something you are aware of, then you have less control over yourself in the way you communicate. One of the overarching issues that managers and executives bring to me is that of communication. 'We don't communicate in our office.' 'We have to learn to communicate better if things are going to change.' There is massive desire and need to communicate better, and understanding the NLP will help you do so.

There is an exercise I often use with groups to help them understand what describes a 'perfect' manager at peak performance. I ask them to come up with as many words or phrases that would apply to such a manager and am never as surprised as they are about the overall nature of the words in the list. A recent list produced is given in Figure 3.1.

The majority of words here are describing an attitude rather than a set of skills. An effective manager or leader has to be open to learning from their staff and themselves. They have to go the extra mile, be prepared to take a risk and at the same time have a sense of humour. They need to be proactive in their in own development as well as encouraging others in theirs. They need to establish and maintain rapport.

Communication is at the heart of much of the management training that is available, whether this be to improve your coaching, interviewing, presentations, negotiating, counselling or project managing. You will be encouraged to think about what you want to say and how you want to say it. When I am involved in assertiveness training, I want delegates to understand the impact of their words and gestures, so they can recognise the difference between assertive, aggressive and passive behaviours. I want them to behave assertively in a way that demonstrates respect for

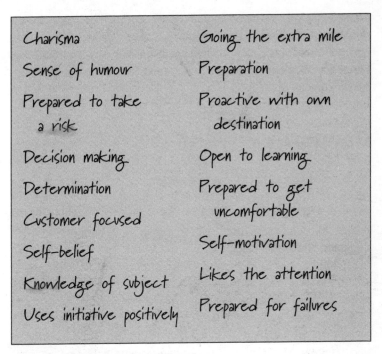

Charisma

Sense of humour

Prepared to take
   a risk

Decision making

Determination

Customer focused

Self-belief

Knowledge of subject

Uses initiative positively

Going the extra mile

Preparation

Proactive with own
   destination

Open to learning

Prepared to get
   uncomfortable

Self-motivation

Likes the attention

Prepared for failures

Figure 3.1: 'Perfect' manager at peak performance

themselves and respect for others. And I want them to be able to do that as well as ask for what they want or put across their point of view. Is it any more or less manipulative to suggest that they will be treated better and reach a win-win solution when they act assertively than to encourage them to use NLP rapport techniques in their communications? For me the key is to understand clearly the intention behind the communication – is it to 'get one over' someone (which I would consider manipulative in the negative sense), or to create an environment in which both parties understand each other and can then opt for the best result?

Within NLP, the skill of rapport is a very important tool. Just like other tools, a screwdriver or hammer for instance, NLP can be used to build and create or to damage and take things apart. It all depends on your *intention* as you use the tool. If your intention with rapport is to help people become the best they can be, and communicate in a way that achieves mutually desirable and beneficial outcomes, others will recognise this and respond positively.

Rapport

'Seek first to understand, then be understood.' Stephen R. Covey

Rapport is the process of building and sustaining a relationship of mutual trust, harmony and understanding. This happens through matching the body language, the behaviour, the words and the breathing of another person or group of people. This might mean sitting down if they are seated, breathing slowly like them or speaking at a fast pace with them. They will have the sense that you are 'with and for' them, rather than against them. The advantage of matching is that the other person recognises at an unconscious level that you understand, value and respect what they are communicating. Rapport is similar to empathy, in that it enables you to appreciate the other person's map of the world, their reality. If you make the effort to be like someone else they will feel more comfortable in their dealings with you. People tend to like people who are like them. If they feel comfortable, then they are more likely to trust you and do business with you. We can also demonstrate rapport by seeing things from someone else's point of view, playing the same tune or getting under their skin in a positive way. It is the ability to relate to others in a way that creates a climate of trust and understanding.

There is a Native American proverb – 'Let me not judge my neighbour until I have walked a mile in his moccasins' – which is a lovely description of rapport. Having an attitude of sincere interest in their 'model of the world' is one of the most respectful ways of creating rapport with people. Asking someone about their interests and finding out what they like to do inside and outside of work helps to build rapport. If it is appropriate, you can find out what they really like or dislike about their job, what their hobbies are, whether they have family and what they have done in previous employment. Very often a person's outside interests are where their passions lie and they will thoroughly enjoy talking about them and having you understand and share their enthusiasm.

Kari came to London to work in the UK branch of a multinational company based in Australia. He was in his own terms 'a boy from the bush', whose interests were surfing, cooking and cricket. When he settled in his new surroundings, he realised he was not in rapport with many of his colleagues and clients. He noticed that in his male-dominated industry, much of the talk was about football – a sport he knew nothing about. He decided to pick a team to support and studied their form and all the ritual that went along with them. After a month he had learned the language and was able to experience the highs and lows with fellow supporters and take part in the banter with those supporting other clubs.

For a new manager, rapport is a vital skill that can be learned or brought into conscious understanding to be fine tuned and then returned to the automatic pilot in the unconscious mind. Learning or revising the skills of rapport will increase your communication choices. Whether you are with colleagues, staff, managers or customers, you can use rapport to understand them better and be better understood. If you exert influence with the use of power without building rapport, you are not influencing but coercing and manipulating. Coercion fails when you lose your powerful position. Rapport works regardless of your status. Using rapport as your method of influence, you will find that people co-operate as a result of exercising choice and free will.

'Rapport is the intelligent approach to influencing, regardless of positional power, whereas power and authority are defaults for people in positions of power who have poor interpersonal skills and little flexibility.' Molden

Of course, when personal power is used wisely, it increases your positional power. When positional power is used wisely, it increases your personal power. However, when either one of them is used improperly, it reduces both your personal authority and positional authority.

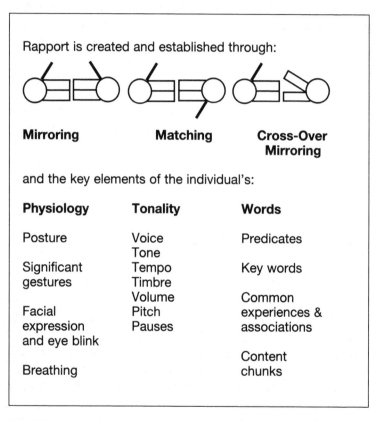

Rapport is created and established through:

Mirroring   **Matching**   **Cross-Over Mirroring**

and the key elements of the individual's:

Physiology	**Tonality**	**Words**
Posture	Voice Tone	Predicates
Significant gestures	Tempo Timbre	Key words
Facial expression and eye blink	Volume Pitch Pauses	Common experiences & associations
Breathing		Content chunks

Figure 3.2: Rapport

As a professional speaker, Seema knows it is crucial to make a good impression whenever she presents. Before taking to the stage, she will have studied relevant websites and visited or spoken to some prospective audience members. She checks if there is any dress code and key words or phrases that apply to the industry. If there is a motto or particular vision that is relevant, she will make sure it is covered it in her speech. She wants to understand as much about her audience as she possibly can so that she can create rapport the minute she makes her entrance. She is able to share 'in' jokes with her audience and knows they will listen to her messages about leadership because they feel comfortable with her, she has shown respect by doing her research and she does not seem to be an outsider. Is that manipulation or attention to detail and doing her job thoroughly?

'When people are like each other, they like each other. Rapport is a process of responsiveness, not necessarily "liking".' Overdurf and Silverthorn

Rapport is created and established through mirroring, matching and cross matching.

Mirroring or matching physiology

Have you ever noticed how some people seem naturally to match body language when they are truly engaged with each other? Their heads move closely together when they are listening intently, they have regular eye contact and they both move away for a rest before they go back into their huddle to engage in their own world of communication. This kind of rapport is often compared to a dance, in which two people glide effortlessly across a ballroom, matching steps, head movements and gestures. They are totally focused on each other and move as one. They have a shared rhythm and timing that is unconscious. When you are naturally in rapport with someone, it makes communication easy and the relationship works well; you do not have to make any effort to match or mirror them in any way, it just happens. However, when you want to be absolutely sure that you will get the best outcome from any interaction you can do so by consciously matching physiology.

To mirror another person, decide on an action or behaviour you want to mirror, then copy that behaviour. If you choose to mirror a head tilt, when the person moves their head, wait a few moments, then move yours to the same angle. The effect should be as though the other person is looking in a mirror. When this is done elegantly, the other person is unaware and quite comfortable with it.

Start by closely observing another person's gestures, posture, facial expressions and breathing, before you change your own to match them. This has an immediate effect on the way that other person perceives you and responds to you. They will feel that there is a genuine connection between you – you are demonstrating your involvement rather than detachment. As you become more practised with this level of rapport, you may find yourself understanding them in a new way. The advantage of matching is that the other person recognises at an unconscious level that you understand and value what they are communicating. It will also help you to join in genuinely with their understanding of the situation.

To make this work and achieve full effects, it needs to be done with respect and sincerity: undermatch and they will not recognise your communication; overmatch and it will seem like mimicry and all rapport is lost. The other person will become uncomfortable at best and suspicious at worst. Start slowly and gradually build up your skill in the art of matching. If someone is sitting, sit down to talk to them; if they are standing do the same. Notice how much eye contact they are comfortable with and match it, notice the angle of their head and the speed of their hand gestures. Are their arms folded or hands clasped, their legs crossed or outstretched, and are they slouched in their chair or sitting straight? When you are matching someone's physiology, take ten to twenty seconds before changing your body – that will seem quite natural to your companion. Remember your intention is to share and understand the other person's experiences of the world, not to be a parrot. At first you might find you go out of rapport with the other person because you are so busy watching their body language, you forget to listen. As with any skill, the more you practice, the easier it will become. You'll soon find you are doing it without trying. It can build a deep sense of trust quickly and it is important that you use it ethically. Mirroring is a powerful way of gaining rapport and can lead to you sharing the other person's experiences. So take care not to mirror people who are in distress or who have severe mental issues.

Become a people watcher. Observe how people interact when they are getting on well and when they are not. Who is in rapport with whom around the water cooler and what occurs when someone joins them? What happens at meetings when there is clear consensus and how does that compare with when there is conflict? Watch people in social situations and decide who is 'out' and who is 'in' rapport. How did you know?

Margaret wanted to practise her rapport skills. She had been invited to attend a client briefing with a training organisation, OT Training, for whom she was the newest associate. She noticed that the client sat with his chin cupped in his hands. He also spoke slowly and at an even pace. When Margaret spoke, she matched the rhythm. Whenever he changed his posture she followed unobtrusively. She enjoyed the meeting and waited for the next instalment. She was delighted when OT's director rang to tell her that they had gained the contract on the proviso that Margaret was lead trainer. The client had felt Margaret's interest and focus on him, which he interpreted as someone he could get along with and who understood his business. For Margaret's part, she found that she had gained a lot of information about the client and his business. By moving into his model of the world, she was allowing herself to be influenced by him and his perspectives.

Cross matching

This is when it is inappropriate to match large gestures such as waving arms. You can cross match using smaller gestures such as tapping your fingers. Or you might want to use one aspect of your behaviour to match a different behaviour in the other person, like nodding your head in time to a series of foot taps, or crossing your legs when they cross their arms.

Matching tonality

At the voice level of rapport you can match tone, tempo, volume pitch and pauses. This is also useful for rapport if you are on the phone and can't see the other person's body language. If someone tends to speak very quietly and you are more naturally a shouter, they will hugely appreciate it if you lower your volume to reach their level. If they tend to talk quite slowly and thoughtfully, they won't respond well to a 'bull in a china shop' approach. Matching someone's rhythm and pace is a key indicator of respect. Children are great at matching tonality and words – it's the way they learn to use language. They pick up the nuances of speech even when they often don't understand the words. When my friend's two-year-said 'I don't think that was called for', she was surprised at the maturity of the tone and intonation her son had used.

Matching language

At the language level of rapport you will be matching the words people use and the stories they choose to impart their information. If someone refers to the latest sales figures as the tip of the iceberg, continue with that theme and ask them what is concealed under the sea. I've noticed that many people use combat metaphors, such as referring to a 'minefield' or 'light the blue touch paper and run'. These are not descriptions that I would usually use but I have consciously added some to my 'war chest' to increase my rapport success.

Matching values

If you can't establish rapport with someone at the values level, your communications will not be effective. That is when attempts at influencing will be met with discomfort and be interpreted as just a trick. You do not have to believe what they do and it is crucial that you acknowledge and respect their views. You need to understand what is important to them and what matters in their lives.

I was working for an organisation, running a series of training days. After negotiating with the head of faculty, we agreed that Day 1 would start with coffee at 9.45 a.m. and the course would officially open at 10 a.m. The subsequent days were set to start at 9 a.m. One of my strong values is punctuality, though I am flexible with timings if adjustments are needed through the day. It soon became clear that punctuality was not important to this particular organisation and people drifted in up to about 10.15 and then asked if we could finish early, as they had other meetings to attend. It took me a while to become more relaxed about the start and finish times – if they wanted to run on shorter days then I could modify the programme and give them work to do outside the training room which they were happy to complete.

One of the most powerful and rewarding ways to create rapport with someone is to accept them just as they are. You may encounter people who have low-self esteem because they have been told from an early age that they are no good and it's not OK to be them. Sometimes they go on to develop unhelpful behaviours which only serve to reinforce the negative messages. When you can accept them just as they are you are sending them a potent message that might allow them to start to feel positive about themselves. If you let them know from a position of rapport that they are worth listening to and are valuable to you and the team, they will reward your recognition and grow in confidence.

To do this most effectively you need first to accept yourself as you are. If you feel uncomfortable about yourself in some way, this will be picked up and limit the degree of rapport you are able to build.

Pacing and leading

Pacing and leading mean communicating with someone from their map of the world (pacing) and then taking them where you want them to go (leading). Rapport is a basic, behavioural signal that you have met someone at their map of the world. The simplest, most effective test for rapport is 'if you lead, they follow'.

Choose a safe situation to practise mirroring an element of someone else's behaviour. When you have mirrored them for a while, and think you are in rapport with them, scratch your nose. If they lift their hand to their face within the next minute or so, congratulate yourself – you have led their behaviour!

This can also be put to use to match strong emotions and help the other person move to a more productive place. When someone is angry and shouting they will not respond well if you quietly ask them to calm down. They may become angrier, think you're patronising them or not even register that you have spoken. Whether you agree with their sentiments or not, they are trying to communicate and have something to tell you. Match them at a slightly lower volume and speed until you can start to slow the pace; as they follow you they will become calmer. They will feel accepted and understood and able to talk coherently about what is bothering them. Equally, if you are with someone who is feeling low and depressed, they will probably be looking down, speaking slowly, if at all, and have very little energy. They are unlikely to change if you bounce in and talk at them very quickly, encouraging them to snap out of it and smell the roses. You will need patience and sensitivity to match their mood before you can start to increase the pace of your speech and encourage them to look upwards, which will lift some of the negative feelings.

Mismatching

Mismatching a value is the quickest and most certain way to destroy rapport.

There may be occasions when you want to break rapport in a discussion or want to switch the focus of the people you are with. Imagine what would happen if you deliberately mismatched the other person(s) involved. By mismatching with your voice, eye contact and body posture, you will subtly interrupt the flow of communication, giving you the opportunity to end the conversation. In most cases people will respond and move away or change direction. An extreme form of mismatching is turning your back. Mismatching is what we do when we say goodbye or signal the end of a conversation.

When Andy is observing delegates practising with role plays, he asks each one to give feedback to the other. On many occasions they start to tell *him* what they liked about their colleague's approach. Andy intentionally mismatches by breaking eye contact and then, by looking at the person to whom he wants them to address their comments, leads them to focus on the delegate requiring information. They then talk to each other as required.

Calibration

Calibration involves using your rapport skills to recognise and interpret different information that is unique to each person. As you study the people around you, they will be giving you clues all the time with their eye movements, breathing, muscle tone and skin colour as to what they are thinking or feeling. As you start to recognise the signs of when someone is feeling receptive or otherwise engaged, you can use this information in deciding what behaviours are appropriate at a given time.

A very obvious example would be noticing the signal someone gives before they cry. It may be that their eyes start to moisten or their lower lip quivers or they bite their lip. Whichever it is, you can anticipate the tears before anything has been said. It is a standing joke in our office that our administrator can tell who is speaking on the other end of the phone just by the way I speak to them. I use different tones and tempos with different callers. How is this useful at work? As you become increasingly aware of these individual and minimal cues from a person, you will be able to recognise a pattern from which to assess their mood. You will also be able to evaluate the effect you are having without just relying on the words.

Calibration check

Find someone at work or outside who is prepared to work with you.

1. Ask them three questions which you know are true for them (Can you drive? Are you over 21? Are you called ...? etc).

   Notice their eye movements, breathing, muscle tone and skin colour as they consider and make their response.

2. Ask them three questions you know to be untrue for them (Are you a concert pianist? Have you been to the moon? etc).

   Notice their eye movements, breathing, muscle tone and skin colour as they consider and make their response.

3. This time they are not to respond verbally and you ask them three questions to which you don't know the answer.

(Have you run a marathon? Do you believe in the supernatural? etc).

Notice their eye movements, breathing, muscle tone and skin colour as they consider their response.

You tell them whether the answer is yes or no.

How did you do? You will find with practice that you notice more pointers to the way people are thinking and processing.

The following case study comes from my colleague Fergus McClelland, director of Vocal Trademark. Dani, a newly promoted senior executive, came to Fergus because her new post gave her responsibility for the whole audit section of the business and a team of 15 junior staff. She loved the work and the challenges it brought, but she was concerned because the junior staff were ignoring her at team meetings. They weren't being rude or nasty, they just didn't seem to hear her. She was having a particular problem with Stuart, who spent most of his time at the meetings looking at the table or floor and saying nothing. When he did speak, his tone was deep and his articulation very measured. He didn't seem to be at all interested.

As Fergus told Dani – 'no-one will take you seriously if you sound like a donkey. You need to work on creating vocal authority, using NLP to help your voice', and that's what she did. Fergus taught her to vary the tone, pitch and speed of her voice so that she could match it to a number of people. He also had her listen to the effect her present 'meetings voice' had and to understand why it might not be catching her team's attention. She lowered her voice tone and then, when wanting to catch Stuart's attention, she slowed her normally quick pace down to match his and made sure she paused regularly to give him the thinking time he needed. Stuart gradually responded to her, developing rapport at the voice level to such an extent that he arrived early to one meeting, looked Dani in the eye when he spoke to her and started volunteering information which was relevant and useful to her part of the business. Dani recently reported back to Fergus that she had attended a meeting at which all the staff were senior to her. She laughed to herself when they asked her to take the chair. The little mouse who six weeks before was being ignored by her juniors was now being asked to take charge of a meeting with her seniors.

Conclusion

- Practise mirroring the micro-behaviours of people on television (chat shows and news interviews are ideal). You may be surprised at how quickly you can become comfortable as you subtly mirror the behaviour of others.
- At the next meeting or networking event you attend, decide to create rapport with at least two people you don't know.
- Remember to start by asking them about themselves and listening to their responses. Keep the conversation focused on them and use all your rapport skills to understand what it is like in their world. Mirror or match their body language, tonality and words. Notice what you can find out about them and what their values are.
- Decide how you can use rapport to increase understanding with your team.

INSTANT TIP

Practice your rapport skills to understand your team better and communicate more effectively with them.

04

How can I interact with people more positively and manage conflict?

'I believe the greatest gift I can conceive of having from anyone is to be seen, heard, understood and touched by them. The greatest gift I can give is to see, hear, understand and touch another person. When this is done, I feel contact has been made.'

Virginia Satir

This chapter is concerned with the clues and cues that help you recognise your own and other people's preferred thinking styles. In NLP these are called 'accessing cues' because they are a collection of signals that let you know how others are accessing information about whatever is happening around them. When you know how someone is processing information, you can work out the best ways to communicate with them.

Representational systems

We use our senses outwardly to perceive the world and inwardly to 're-present' experiences to ourselves. In NLP the ways we take in, store and code information in our minds are known as representational systems. Referred to collectively as VAKOG, these are; *Visual* – what we see; *Auditory* – what we hear; *Kinaesthetic* – what we feel and touch; *Olfactory* – what we smell; and *Gustatory* – what we taste. As we think about the world around us, we do so using pictures, sounds, feelings, tastes and smells. Visual, auditory and kinaesthetic are known as the primary systems, while olfactory and gustatory are often included in the kinaesthetic sense because they can serve as powerful and immediate links to the sights, sounds and pictures associated with them. On a daily basis, we use all the senses available to us, but there will be some priority order – a preferred sense that we access more 'naturally' and use more often.

The skill is to recognise, without judging, the systems being used and to work with them. Excellent communicators do this instinctively. They move around the representational systems to include and reach each member of their audience. In any presentation when they do not know someone, whether it be to one person or a number of people, they will use all the three main representational systems (visual, auditory and kinaesthetic) to ensure that everyone can either see, hear or make sense of the points they are making. In the same way as our map of the world represents only part of the territory, so our preferred representational system is only part of the picture, one sound bite or feels incomplete.

Over time we develop preferences for one of the representational systems and will tend to use that more often. In different contexts we may well use the other systems too; it is just that we become more comfortable and practised in one of the three. In any discussion where different systems are being used exclusively, a translator may be needed.

When Peter, whose preferred system is auditory, was *explaining* to Nikki about the latest marketing scheme, he knew he was way behind schedule. He couldn't think how to make up the time because he was interrupted and had to *listen* to an internal voice reminding him how late he was. Nikki, whose preferred system is visual, wanted to *show* Peter a quick way to help clarify the issue. She had a diagram that *signposted* his best route. Marek, whose preferred system is kinaesthetic, was becoming increasingly *agitated* with both of them and decided to *grasp* the nettle and mediate. He *showed* Nikki Peter's timetable and perception of the predicament. He *told* Peter what it *sounded* like to Nikki. Marek became more *relaxed* as he *sensed* a more constructive *atmosphere* between them.

Which is your preferred system? Think back to your last meeting or team briefing and write down or record the words to describe it, or draw a diagram. Which was the first sense that came into your head? Now consider your last customer meeting, with internal or external customers, and repeat the process. Finally, think about your most recent experience of moving house and write or record your thoughts. Is you bias towards visual, auditory or kinaesthetic thinking? Did you recognise your second and third preferences?

Predicates

Predicates are the words we use that differentiate between the representational systems. We use language to communicate what we are thinking about and our, usually unconscious, choice of words reflects the way we think. Our words indicate which representational system we are using. Consider how you or your colleagues respond to the events after a team brief. How do they like to consolidate the information from the meeting and ensure they make the most of it? Are any of these three familiar?

After the meeting, and in visual mode, Sasha would like to *see* a copy of the minutes *written* down or in an email for her to *read*.

In auditory mode, Denise would prefer to *hear* what happened or *talk* it over with someone else, particularly the section that wasn't on her *wavelength*. If Phil wanted to *touch* base after the meeting to *weigh up* his and others' *feelings* about the meeting, he would be in kinaesthetic mode. These three could have a fascinating or frustrating post-meeting discussion if they became stuck in their preferred system. You might want to consider whether you already have a way of making sure all three needs are met or whether you tend only to accommodate colleagues with same primary system as yourself.

Take the time to listen to and note your colleague's words as often as you can. When you recognise their preferred systems, you may understand them better. Are you speaking the same *language*? Do you see the same *pictures*? Are you as *hands on* as they are? You may well find that these change depending on the context, so try a number of different situations to check until you have a better understanding of where their bias is. Different people will have different responses. None is right or wrong, they just are. It is important to remember that these provide information and are not a way to label people. I know one very visually biased person who used to cringe every time they heard a kinaesthetic say things like 'touch base', or 'run this past you'. Now they are more inclined to relax, settle down and enjoy collecting information. If you can identify the preferences of your staff and colleagues, you can start to communicate with them with words that will be best suited to them and that will make perfect sense to them!

Predicate identifier examples – words

Visual	Auditory	Kinaesthetic	Ol/Gus
see	hear	feel	aroma
hazy	dissonant	creepy	bland
insight	harmony	relaxed	bouquet
glare	whine	agitate	sour
transparent	monotonous	smooth	acrid

Predicate identifier examples – phrases

Visual	Auditory	Kinaesthetic	Ol/Gus
looks good to me	same wavelength	feels solid	fresh as a daisy
outside my picture	can't hear myself think	heated debate	smell a rat
seeing eye to eye	singing our tune	wet blanket	a sweet person
shed some light on...	clear explanation	sticky situation	get the flavour of ...
show me what you mean	accent on success	smooth operator	whiff of success
	rings bells ...	common ground	swallow your pride
has a blind spot	turn a deaf ear	tackle head on	it's not palatable

You are more likely to gain rapport with a person who thinks in the same way as you and you discover this by listening to the words they use. You don't have to agree with them – you are wanting to let them know you are on the same wavelength, seeing eye to eye or getting a feel for their ideas.

Eye accessing movements

People move their eyes in systematic directions depending on which representational system they are accessing. These movements are known as eye accessing cues. The diagram below shows the processing that is happening when people move their eyes in a certain direction.

Were you ever told 'look at me when I am talking to you'? This can be one of the most difficult instructions to follow. The last place most people want to focus their eyes is directly at the person speaking to them, especially if they are trying to access information with which to respond. The way you move your eyes is another indicator of the representational system you are using. Research in NLP suggests that people using the visual representational system tend to look upwards or defocus, those using auditory look sideways and those using kinaesthetic look downwards.

Further refinement indicates that, in general, a right-handed person looks to the left when they are recalling a past event or experience one that is left behind in their memory and up to the right when they are creating an imagined outcome for the first time. For some left-handed people the patterns are reversed. As this is a generalised model, check your observations in as many ways as you can. Use calibration (see Chapter 3) as a way of observing each person's unique cues; even if they do not fit the general rules, they will move their eyes consistently in a way that represents their thinking system.

As you go through the following exercises you may find you respond differently from the suggested eye movements. Don't despair, you are not wrong or strangely built, just unique. Discover your individual patterns.

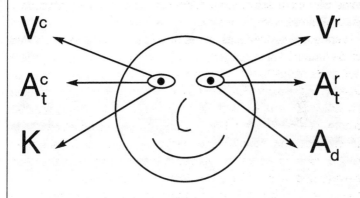

EYE ACCESSING MOVEMENTS
FOR A 'NORMALLY ORGANIZED'
RIGHT-HANDED PERSON

V^c	**V^r**
Visual constructed images	Visual remembered images
(Eyes Defocused and Unmoving also indicate Visual Accessing)	
A^c	**A^r**
Auditory constructed sounds	Auditory remembered sounds
K	**A^d**
Kinesthetic – sensations & feelings	Auditory sounds or words self talk

Figure 4.1: Eye accessing movements

Visual

A person using visual accessing cues will answer the questions below after locating a picture in their mind. Invite someone to ask you these questions and to note where your eyes go. Then swap round with them and note their eye movements. You don't need to speak the answers, what matters is *how* you arrive at them. Analysing eye movements takes practice and over time you will notice patterns more easily.

> What did your first work space look like? *(eyes up and left)*
> Imagine your MD with pink hair and wearing a bright orange suit? *(eyes up and right)*

At work

A person with a preferred visual representation system will want to see diagrams and charts and be more likely to use flip charts or PowerPoint to show what they are thinking. You will have less success with them if you only *tell* them your ideas, without illustration. They may need to see things in writing and prefer email to telephone calls. You might want to ask them: 'Have you tried looking at it from this perspective?'

Auditory

When people are thinking in sounds, their eyes move across towards the left ear for remembered sounds and towards the right ear for imagined sound.

> Recite your two times table? *(eyes across left)*
> How would your voice sound under water? *(eyes across right)*

At work

Those with a preferred auditory representation system will want to discuss issues rather than receive them in print. They like to talk and often 'think out loud' as they gather their thoughts. So much so that they may talk through and change their ideas a number of times until they are clear for themselves. Auditories work more efficiently in quiet atmospheres – so they can 'hear themselves think'. They tend to prefer the phone to email and are probably comfortable with answerphones. You might want to know: 'What's your story of the events?'

Kinaesthetic

If someone's eyes look down and to the right, they are processing in kinaesthetic mode and this puts them in touch with either their internal emotions or an external tactile feeling. They may also be in olfactory or gustatory mode.

> How do you react when you are angry?
> How would you feel in sinking sand? } *(eyes down and right)*
> Think of your favourite scent.
> What does ice cream taste like?

At work

Kinaesthetics will start with their 'gut feelings' in the way they react to different situations. They will want to work out how they feel about an issue before being ready to discuss or look at it. They often process at an intuitive level and may not have a rational argument to support their ideas, they 'just have sense' about things. They tend to foster good relationships at work because they can pick up underlying and unspoken feelings. They want to experience and test things out before they feel comfortable with them. You might want to suggest: 'Can we scratch that idea and make a fresh start?'

Internal dialogue

When people are in conversation with themselves, having an 'internal dialogue', then their eyes will tend to look down and to the left. This is another system of thinking and can take longer to process before responding. It is often associated with people being 'deep in thought'.

> In quiet times, what do you find yourself thinking about?
> Repeat silently 'I am who am I and I am fine'.
> } *(eyes down and left)*

At work

The key to communicating with a person using this mode is to give them plenty of time. They are literally talking things over with themselves and can become confused or frustrated if you keep asking supplementary questions through your impatience. You might want to check: 'What are you telling yourself when you consider the pros and cons of this decision?'

Think up your own questions to check how other people's eyes give information about their primary representational system and increase your skill of responding in the same way. Note the common words or phrases that they use and you will find you rapidly increase your own vocabulary and translation skills. Revisit the calibration exercise and add eye movements and predicates to your analysis.

Note that these are generalisations. Not everyone fits neatly into them. What you may notice is that although someone looks in an unexpected direction they are likely to be consistent in their eye movements, so you can learn to recognise their system. Remember to notice their predicates, too, for confirmation. In many cases you will find that reverse direction works for someone who is left-handed.

Body language

The gestures you make, the qualities in your voice and the way you breathe are further indicators of the representational system you are using at any time. They may be the first aspects you notice or the final check after you have heard the predicates and detected the eye movements.

When you think about it, it makes perfect sense that conflict can arise when people are processing information in different ways and don't recognise each others' preferences. As you increase your skill, and can interpret the mismatches, you will go a long way towards creating a more harmonious team. Your first job is to know your own primary system and decide who in your team has a matching preference. Do you find them easier to deal with than other team members? Do the same with your secondary system

	Visual	Auditory	Kinaesthetic
Voice	speak quickly and higher pitch than Auditory or Kinaesthetic	clear expressive rich and resonant	deeper, slower, with pauses
Head	head up, shoulder muscles tense	well balanced or leaning to one side	angled downwards
Breath	centred high in chest area and shallow	evenly over whole chest area	deep and low in abdomen
Gestures	exaggerated sit/stand erect gestures upwards	move rhythmically touching ears or near ears lips move	relaxed posture, with rounded shoulders

and then the one you tend to use less often. It is astounding how many serious breaks in communication can be fixed once you can translate the different 'languages' to restore harmony and smooth running and have a clear picture in the office.

Have you ever been distracted by someone clicking their pen or tapping their fingers on the desk while you are working near them or talking to them? Maybe you are a pen clicker or tapper yourself. Or perhaps you are disrupted by the whistling coming from your auditory-biased colleague at the other side of the office. Does your visually preferred manager disturb you with her doodling as you try to explain an idea or concept? The fascinating thing is that what they are doing is concentrating from their preferred thinking mode. Once you understand that, you can be more sympathetic and less distracted. One of my colleagues gives out soft 'stress balls' to the kinaesthetics in her training room, so they can fully concentrate in silence. I don't know what she does with the whistlers!

I was working with Sandy, who was experiencing a lot of problems with a couple of team members. She had sent round an email asking everyone to be more observant when checking some complicated orders that were coming in. On the whole, all were doing well but a few mistakes were getting through. At least that was her understanding of the email she sent. The email in fact read:

> Be more observant with F487 orders, some that
> look questionable are getting through. Thanks.

Having visual as her primary representational system, Sandy liked to use email, which was quick and to the point. Dan and Gabby disagreed. They felt that Sandy was picking on them and this was just one more example of how she rubbed them up the wrong way. They were both prepared to down tools and go. Sandy was furious. Whenever she asked them to do anything, they took ages to respond and, to her, seemed very slow and deliberate in what they did. Once she understood that they were kinaesthetic in their thinking, she practised re-wording her emails and made a point of telling them that she had not intended putting them under pressure. When she talked to them she slowed her speech and gave them space to reply. The email that would have suited all staff was:

> F487 orders flowing through well overall.
> Looking and sounding good. Please check all
> stay error free. Thanks.

All she needed was three more words to satisfy all three systems.

Perceptual positions

As a manager, when you find yourself having a different opinion from someone who works for (or with) you, or you seem stuck in your communication, it can be very valuable to change your position (literally and figuratively) and take different views of the situation. This is sometimes called second guessing. If you can understand their thinking and work out their positive intentions, then you have added knowledge to take you forward. Assuming the presupposition that 'people come to work to do their best', then there is a useful tool that helps you find out what is stopping them doing just that. This NLP technique is called 'perceptual positions'. It enables you to appreciate someone else's point of view more fully, helps to reduce tension and enables you to respond more resourcefully. As a manager you can employ perceptual positions to get a deeper insight into the staff who report to you, and greater awareness of your relationship with them. Utilising perceptual positions makes a powerful contribution to the management of the inevitable discord, disagreement and conflict that can be so apparent in the busy modern workplace. In situations where you feel there is little or no understanding or progress, perceptual positions can provide a way of developing understanding and creating new choices. The idea behind perceptual positions is that you consider the issue first from your own position and gain deeper comprehension of your stance on the issue. Then you move into the other person's world and assess the situation as if you were them. From that position the argument or action taken makes perfect sense. Finally, you take the position of the detached observer. This is the 'fly on the wall' position – you have none of the emotional investment of the other two positions, just a healthy interest in finding out what is going on between one and two.

The three basic perceptual positions

1st position: self – This is your reality; how you see, hear and feel about the situation. You think in terms of what matters to you. 'As far as I'm concerned …'; 'My take on this is …'

2nd position: other – This is the other person's reality; how it would look, sound and feel if you were them. When you say 'from where I'm standing …', you are using 'I' to mean the other person because, for this moment, you are them and discovering how they are affected.

3rd position: observer – The detached observer. How might this appear to someone who is not involved? You can watch both parties interact and notice what is happening without experiencing either person's emotions.

Within companies you can become so involved in production or service delivery (1st position, your map) that you may not know whether your efforts are being channelled in the most productive way. Your many customers will have their own views about your service and you may find it useful to gain insight into their map through the second perceptual position. Ask yourself: 'What would I think about delivery times and quality if I were one of my customers?' The third, observer's position enables you to assess the interactions between 1 and 2 without any of the emotional interference. Imagine how useful it would be to know what's going on in the minds of your staff, your customers, your bosses and your competitors.

Practise perceptual positions for yourself and notice how they help the situation you choose.

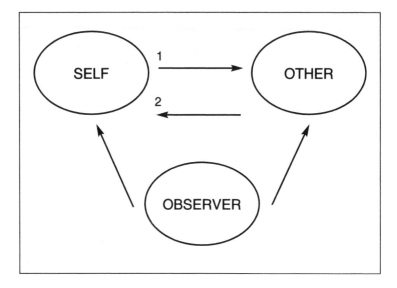

Figure 4.2: Perceptual positions

Exercise
- Think of an unsatisfactory situation between you and someone else.
- Put three sheets of paper, labelled 'self', 'other' and 'observer' on the floor. Make them equidistant as in Figure 4.2.
- Stand on the 'self' sheet, facing the 'other' and recognise how you experience the situation you have chosen. What do you see, hear or feel? Decide what you would like to say to the other person. Then move away.
- Stand on the 'other' sheet and imagine you are that person looking at the 'self'. Recognise how you, as the other person, might experience the interaction. What do you see, hear or feel? Decide what you would like to say to 'self'? Then move away.

- Step onto the 'observer' sheet and look at 'self' and 'other'. From this neutral position, notice what is happening. What is or isn't being achieved? Remember that you do not take sides, this is the place for objective assessment. If you notice any emotions as you stand on 'observer' check whether they belong to 'self' or 'other'. 'Observer' is a neutral position. Then move away.
- Move back to 'self' and repeat the stages as many times as you need to gain full information and insight.
- Decide what you will do as a result of your new understanding.

Perceptual positioning is also useful when you are considering launching a new product or have a proposal to make or checking the 'fit' of an outcome. By thinking in the following terms you will be able to broaden your approach and increase your flexibility:

- How will this look from the customers', suppliers', manufacturers', employees' points of view?
- What would this sound like to our overseas colleagues?
- How might other staff feel about this approach?

Create some of your own questions to help you understand as many views as possible of any situation.

The following case study comes from my colleague Simon Hazeldine, author of *Bare Knuckle Selling*.

Following a reorganization, I had been given a new sales team. Some of the members of the team didn't like the changes that had taken place in their working practices as a result of the re-organization. Bill (who was regarded by other members of the team as the 'top dog' due to his age and experience) was openly hostile towards me. During early team meetings Bill's hostile comments and behaviour were influencing the other members of the team in a negative way.

After one meeting I decided to go through a perceptual positions exercise, adopting first position to consider the situation from my perspective and then second position to consider his. After adopting his physiology, I began to initially perceive the hostility and feel that a significant issue was the fact that I was so much younger than Bill. However, as I explored further it became apparent that underlying the hostility was a strong feeling of fear. Bill was scared of me, or at least scared of what I represented. As I then shifted to adopt third position, I could see that some of my behaviour (I was doing my very best to be a dynamic, make it happen, thrusting, young sales manager!) was actually exacerbating the feelings of fear that Bill was experiencing. With this enriched perspective I was able to modify my behaviour.

The next week I was accompanying Bill as he visited some of his customers. Over coffee I concentrated on building some rapport between us. Once I felt that sufficient connection had been established, I started to gently probe into Bill's thoughts about the re-organization. I continued to ask questions, encouraging him to share his thoughts and opinions. After about twenty minutes Bill suddenly said that he was nervous of all the new young salespeople being brought into the sales force and that due to his age he was worried that the company would want to get rid of the 'old stagers' like him, and, as Bill described it, 'put him out to pasture'. If this happened before he had planned it would adversely affect his pension.

Whilst I couldn't give Bill any guarantees about what may or may not happen in the future, I did assure him that to my knowledge the company had no such plans and that I most certainly did not have any 'hidden agenda'. I had noted that Bill's language was peppered with comments like 'being put out to pasture' and 'you can't teach an old dog new tricks' so deliberately started to introduce similar expressions into my language.

As we sat drinking our coffee I reframed Bill's comments about 'old stagers' by saying, 'Bill you must have been a member of more sales teams than almost anyone else in the company and like a good football team you need a mix of experience and youth, don't you? Having some "new blood" in the team is very important. We both know that we need the new ideas and raw energy of the younger staff. However, we also both know that they are often "wet behind the ears" and need someone with enough wisdom and experience, to "smooth their rough edges"! They need someone who has enough years "under their belt" to "show them the ropes". I need someone to be the foundation of my team, someone who is "solid as a rock". I need someone to help to make this team the very best sales team in the company. We are a team and I can't do this on my own. I'm fairly new to being a sales manager myself and I know I need a "right hand man" who I can count on. And I am hoping that the person is you.'

In the next sales meeting Bill, who seemed very taken with his new role as the 'foundation' of the team, was a different person – even to the extent of taking one or two of the team members to task for their negative attitude!

Throughout my time leading the team Bill continued to be highly supportive, often taking new salespeople 'under his wing', as he put it, taking the lead on new initiatives and ways of working, and being the most solid foundation in a team that a young inexperienced sales manager could ever have wished for.

As a manager when you find yourself with a different opinion to someone who works for (or with) you, appreciating their point of view more fully helps to reduce tension and enables you to respond more resourcefully. Utilising perceptual positions make a powerful contribution to the management of the inevitable discord, disagreement and conflict that can be so apparent in the busy modern workplace. This principle can be easily applied to any work relationship – colleagues, people in your team you don't get on with, people you need to persuade and, of course, your boss!

Conclusion

Introducing change in the workplace is more acceptable if you can first match and pace the parties involved. Some basic research about how best to manage information saves time and conflict later on. People like and feel understood by people who are like themselves. So consider: would your colleagues want to see a written account of your proposals, would they rather talk them over or would they prefer time to grasp and sense the nature of your ideas?

Decide how you might approach the following situations in each of the three main representational systems. Write or record a prepared statement for each.

	Visual	*Auditory*	*Kinaesthetic*
Recruitment interview	We've looked at your CV, where do you see yourself in five years?	It looks like you have wide experience, tell me about ...	In which of your last jobs did you feel most settled?
Closing a meeting			
Staff briefing			
Appraisal			
Customer meeting			
Introduce new rotas			

INSTANT TIP

Check whether disagreements or conflicts can be resolved through recognition of representational systems.

05

How do I make the transition from team member to team manager?

The good news is that moving from team member to team manager will not be the first change you have ever made at work or outside. According to the NLP presupposition, 'you have all the resources you need', that means, if you have done it before, you can do it again, and successfully now. I am often reminded that we take old changes for granted and forget that once they were deemed difficult and sometimes insurmountable, but we got there. One of the earliest achievements for most of us was to make the transition from being fed to feeding ourselves. I don't know if you can remember how complicated it seemed to balance food on a strange implement like a spoon and then be expected to navigate it to your mouth, which was only a small space in the whole of your face. I certainly don't know how long it took me, but I look on with wonder at the level of concentration and skill that it takes a baby to manage this task. Happily, most of us can now send food to our mouths without even thinking about it, and yet it wasn't always so. When you look back at your career, maybe even remember your very first day at work, there will have been so much going on around you, so much to remember, all of which is now second nature to you. You will soon feel the same about being team manager.

NLP is all about change and how to create the life you want for yourself. One of NLP's leading thinkers, Robert Dilts, suggests that there are six levels in which to understand change, learning and communication. He terms them 'logical levels', because they fit together in a logical, hierarchical way. This enables you to consider change from the abstract 'big picture' level and chunk down to the more specific 'detail' level. The NLP logical levels are very useful for assisting with or understanding change from an individual, social or organisational point of view.

Logical levels of change	
Connectedness / purpose	Who else is involved and how does it affect them?
Identity / mission	Who am I when I am doing this?
Beliefs / values	Why am I doing this?
Capabilities	How do I do this, what are my skills?
Behaviour	What am I doing?
Environment	Where am I doing it?

Dilts suggests that any changes made at the higher levels will have a greater influence on you than those made at the lower levels. The most important factor for effective change is to recognise at which level you are stuck in any particular context. Do you need to change your behaviour to become a more effective manager? Perhaps you still think of yourself as a team member, which is an identity level issue. Have you ever heard anyone say: 'I can't believe they've promoted me'? This would suggest they are challenged at the belief level and will need to find ways of being convinced that their promotion is totally believable and deserved.

There are some aspects of your life that are so much easier to change than others. One person will think nothing of re-locating regularly to progress in their job – an environmental change. Another may be just as happy to keep changing the job they are doing – a behavioural change. A third might want to be a perpetual student, collecting qualifications and competencies – a change at the capabilities level. To make these changes easily depends on your beliefs, your identity and the broader systems to which you belong.

Once you are more familiar with the different levels, you will be able to understand and match to those which other people are operating too. The logical levels are also relevant to companies. If the directors of a company introduce change at one level which is not in line with the thinking of the rest of the work force, they are unlikely to experience smooth reorganisation. This is particularly relevant in mergers and take-overs, where there are different values or beliefs which require different ways of operating. If these issues are not addressed, the new business will lose valued staff who feel uncomfortable with the new regime. The new company needs to have a clear identity to share with the amalgamating groups. Staff at all strata can fear being 'taken over' and pushed into an alien identity. If the new identity is considered during the merger process, it can make transition much smoother. This also applies to the integration of departments within a company.

The logical levels can help you develop greater flexibility in the way you think about all aspects of your life. The table above gives you an idea of the questions that help you to check which level or levels are problematical and how to address the issues they reveal. Where things are already going well, you can use the levels as a guide to making your situation even better as they extend your awareness of what in your life is working for you.

The description below explains each logical level and how it might relate to you and your business.

Connectedness / purpose

This level refers to the larger system of which you are a part. In a metaphysical sense it is understanding your purpose in whatever you do in the world around you. This is *your* innermost sense of yourself. This level gives you a sense of whether or not you are fulfilled in what you are doing. If your feelings are strong at this level, you may only need to make minor adjustments elsewhere. If this is where you feel unease, then you might need to make changes across the board.

At this level you would be answering the questions: 'Why am I here?', 'How does this fit into the scheme of my life?'

Whatever changes you make in your life are likely to affect those around you and will include consideration of your higher purpose. Your decisions about the type of work you would prefer to do will be influenced by the systems to which you want to belong. Given the choice, most people work in settings that complement their ethical position, otherwise they can find themselves at odds with the company mission. Companies that attend to their bigger system are concerned about the world in which they do business. To this end, some insurance companies have 'ethical portfolios' which are committed to investing only in projects that make minimal demands on the world's resources.

Identity

Your identity is a description of *who* you think you are, at any given time and in any given role. It is often conveyed in the labels you give yourself. In many cases they have a qualitative element: 'I am a financial wizard.' As you travel through life, your sense of yourself changes at this identity level and influences some of the options to which you allow yourself to be open. Your identity level can therefore be empowering or restricting of your development. You can enhance someone else's self-esteem by giving them positive feedback at the identity level: 'You are an excellent team leader.'

At this level you would be answering the question: 'Who am I when I am doing this?'

You will have a number of different identities, depending on the context. Think about your identity when you attend a meeting. Are you the chairperson, the minute taker, an expert, a representative, a participant, an observer, an ex officio member, a volunteer, or a combination of some of these? When you go to a family gathering are you a parent, child, brother, sister, aunt, uncle etc? Whichever way you describe yourself passes on a message to those around you. I am often fascinated to hear how people introduce themselves to the rest of the delegates on a training course: 'I'm just a ... ' It is delightful when their sense of identity has changed to: 'I am a successful and valued leader of the team.'

'It's just the way I am.' 'This is how God intended me to be.' There is often a quite fixed sense of self behind these statements. Some people are frightened that a new identity might fundamentally alter their perception of themselves or others' perceptions of them. This, of course, ties in with their beliefs too. The company identity gives employees and customers a clear idea of what to expect from them. Where there is a strong figure head as founder, they will often incorporate their identities and values into the company. This was certainly the case with Anita Roddick when she founded the Body Shop. The franchises expect to employ staff who have a similar identity and beliefs. They are clearly all working towards the same outcomes.

There is sometimes a challenge when there is a dichotomy between the identity presented to the customer and its non-application to staff. 'A company that cares ...' may not be consistent in its treatment of its staff. This can percolate through to the way staff treat customers and the company identity becomes meaningless. Working with logical levels can uncover these inconsistencies and, in this case, enable the identity to be revisited and followed through for everyone.

I have worked in companies where there is a clear demarcation between staff and managers with few promotion opportunities from within. Staff are staff and can't expect to be anything else. Those who buy into that identity can become stuck without advancement, those who don't will often leave. The identity of such a company is: 'we are a company who expect all senior staff to have external working experience.'

Beliefs / values

In Chapter 2 we considered the influence of beliefs on the way you think, your feelings and how you behave as a result. At the logical level of beliefs, you are working with what you believe to be true and this forms the basis for daily action. Some beliefs are handed down through families and go unchallenged from generations: they can take the form of 'sayings' and are very powerful. 'You can't teach an old dog new tricks', 'If it tastes bad, it's doing you good', 'Learning happens everywhere', 'Life begins at forty'. Can you think of any that are still around for you? Are they helpful or ready to be jettisoned?

Your values are the criteria against which you make decisions. They are the attributes that are important to you in the way you live your life. These could include: loyalty, liberty or honesty. Your beliefs support and reinforce your values. You have to believe that you can change in order to make changes at any of the logical levels.

At this level you would be answering the questions: 'Why am I doing this?', 'Why is this important to me?'

Beliefs can promote or inhibit your personal growth. Henry Ford is reported to have said: 'Whether you think you can or whether you think you can't, you're probably right.' Many beliefs are conveyed in thoughts; they represent your opinion more than firm facts. You tend to notice information that reinforces them and delete the opposite view. When a colleague, Ronny, was complimented on his presentation to the staff group, he brushed it aside as a fluke. He didn't believe he could make presentations. When one person suggested he could have used more audio visual aids, he accepted that as part of his 'inability' belief.

Have you ever noticed the passion and zeal in brand new companies? People work exceptionally long hours for relative little financial gain. The rewards they are getting stem from the firm and shared belief in what they are doing. There is a captivating energy that maintains momentum. As with identity, it is important that the company's beliefs about customers as human beings should also be reflected in the beliefs about staff.

There are many limiting beliefs around in the area of new technology. People who for years have managed with a typewriter or secretarial assistance, now find a PC on their desk. The beliefs that stop them from using the machinery are based in lack of confidence or fear of the new. Such beliefs include: 'I can't work machines', 'It's too complicated, I'll break it', 'I'm too old to learn'. Contrast that with: 'I thrive on anything new', 'I can handle it'.

A company's values provide the codes of practice for the work force, for example, equal opportunities and environmental policies. There is obvious discord when the company displays such policies but does not actually believe them or behave in a way that supports them.

Capabilities

Your capabilities are the resources that you have available to you as skills and qualities. They may be formally recognised through standards, qualifications and competencies and will be demonstrated by the strategies you use. Many of your capabilities are processes that you perform regularly and in many cases are automatic and habitual. Repeatable management procedures are at the capabilities level and include coaching and appraising.

At this level you would be answering the questions: 'How am I doing this?' 'What are my skills?'

Managing is a skill that you can learn. You will already have many of the competences you need to be a successful manger and there are many different ways you can learn and attain new skills as you career develops. Being a manager means that you also have to identify your team's capability gaps and requirements. Once you have learned a new set of skills you might want to consider how you incorporate them. It is great to return from a counselling skills course fired with enthusiasm. If you insist that everyone tells how they feel all the time, they may react in a negative way. You are only part of the way to absorbing the capability that ensures appropriate use of your counselling skills.

Companies that want to restructure in some way will succeed if they have attained the necessary capabilities on the way. It may seem a small jump to go from being a photographic studio specialising in portraits to a retail film developer. You may be able to develop your own pictures, you also need to know how to handle different types of films and a different customers. Your accounting skills and staffing needs will be changed.

Behaviours

Your behaviours are what you do, what you say and what those around you observe or hear. They are the external representation of your capabilities, beliefs, identity and connectedness. If you have an outcome to aim for, you will be greatly helped by considering the actions you will take to get there. The Chinese have a saying, 'a journey of a thousand miles starts with a single step'. Action is key to moving your outcomes towards reality. Behaviours can be easily learned through copying significant role models around us. Modelling, which was discussed in Chapter 1 is one of the key NLP skills and was used as a major part of NLP's creation. Bandler and Grinder wanted to know what the key thinkers *did* that made them excellent.

At this level you would be answering the question: 'What am I doing?'

What are you doing to achieve your outcomes, both personal and work related? You can set yourself behavioural tasks that will enhance your development. You have been promoted to team leader – a new identity – so what will you do differently as a result. You will be expected to run team meetings and spend time with each member of the team. You will need to make decisions with more authority than before.

What new behaviours do you have to perform since taking this post?

Behaviours are sometimes confused with identity and capability which, when commented on, can damage a person's confidence and competence. Failing an exam doesn't mean that you are stupid or useless at studying, but, if it is taken at those levels, you are unlikely to seek feedback as to how you can improve. When you are giving or receiving feedback, consider it at this level of what you do, not the identity level – who you are. 'You failed this exam but you have passed many other testing situations in your life.'

Companies behave in many different ways to let the outside world know they exist. They conduct market research surveys and advertising campaigns, they sponsor local charities and send out promotional material to prospective and existing customers. There are set or agreed behaviours that need to be actioned for many company procedures, from allocating petty cash to promotions. These behaviours are lovingly referred to as 'red tape'.

Sometimes you can change an unwanted behaviour for a short period of time, and then you find you have returned to it. If the new behaviour is not in alignment with the your beliefs and values or identity, the higher level will override the lower level. For change at the behaviour level to be long term, the desired behaviour change must either be in alignment with the higher levels or the change must take place at a high level, i.e. identity, and then the behaviour will follow.

I was working with a newly promoted police inspector who was struggling with a couple of his sergeants. They were finishing shifts early and not completing all their paperwork, which he ended up doing himself. His challenge was that they were his mates, with whom he went fishing, and all the families socialised together. He didn't want to discipline them because he valued their friendship. Once we talked about the identity level of being an inspector who had obligations to the force and the rest of his team, he psyched himself up and had words with both of them. His behaviour at work changed and so did theirs. A lovely postscript was that they responded to his demands for change with a laugh and the admission that they wondered how long it would be before he brought them to task.

Environment

This refers to everything that is outside you; where you are, the people you are with, your home, your work, our surroundings.

At this level you would be answering the question: 'Where and with whom?'

Individual implications

Your choice of where to live will be influenced by your beliefs and your identity. If you have to move home, you would also consider environmental level factors such as schools, public transport, green space, distance from friends etc. Where you go and what you do socially can all be considered at the environment level. Environment can also include new technology and gadgets – the aids you have around you. Your ability to use them relates back to the capabilities and beliefs level. In companies, the comfort and safety of your surroundings make a big difference to how well you work and how satisfied you are. Many people will tolerate a poor working environment if they have good relationships with their work colleagues. For others the office environment is crucial to effective working. I have noticed a huge difference in the atmosphere and start to a training day, depending on whether I am in a room with natural light or a basement with no windows, too many people for the room and nowhere to go for a break.

The following case study comes from my colleague Andrew Whitaker, an executive coach with People Development Works.

Andrew was working with Darren, a likeable, hard-working man, who had been with Millers for three years. He was popular with the majority of his fellow workers, had a good relationship with his clients and his performance was always above average. Promotion seemed the next logical step of his career. When Darren received the news he was to become a 'team leader', a middle management position with a team of 12 people in his sphere of influence, he was over the moon.

Darren was very ambitious and dreamt of having the best, most successful team in the company. On his first day he organised a meeting with everybody. Darren introduced himself and told everyone about his vision of theirs being the best team in the company. He emphasised that he wanted everyone to contribute and succeed within the team. Everyone agreed, smiled and nodded. Unfortunately, after three months the team figures were no better, the revenue was the same, profit had increased only slightly and he still had a member going sick all the time.

Andrew decided to work with Darren at the beliefs, values and behaviour levels to help him reach his goal.

'First of all your people have got to want to be number one, I'm not talking about saying they want to be number one, they have really got to feel it in their hearts, you have to light the fire within them, energise them, get them excited about what's possible and then give them a massive reason why being number one is for them.'

Once Andrew had explained and worked through the values logical level, Darren was ready to do the same with his team. He emphasised how people's values have to come from them. Many companies come up with company values and mission statements in the boardroom, they then hold a company event and tell everyone that these are the company values, this is how you will behave from now on. That just doesn't work. People will nod their heads and agree because nobody wants to rock the boat (just like Darren's team had done), but values are sacred and people's opinions have to be respected. The team were delighted to be consulted. They created and agreed the following values:

- Every client to be treated as their only client.
- Openness and honesty.
- Best practice. Share all good working practice.
- Give every call 100 per cent.
- Maximise each call and sales opportunity.
- Respect for everyone we come into contact with.
- Success for myself and the team.
- Fun and enjoyment.

Mission statement: 'To be the very best we can today, tomorrow and always with a big smile on our faces and desire in our hearts.'

As a result, the team seemed to have a new energy about them, a drive that hadn't been there before and the team seemed happier. Their behaviours changed, they brought each other little gifts for successes, they seemed to have adopted certain roles which they solely concentrated on rather than doing a little bit of everything each and operating as individuals; they really seemed to come together as a well-oiled machine. They were having fun, fun with a purpose.

The last time Andrew contacted Darren he found out that the team had reached position two in their company league table in just three months. Darren was happy, Darren's boss was happy, and the team were very happy, chasing world class status.

Think about your new management role. Were you delighted to accept because you have always imagined yourself as a manager (identity)? Or are you a little apprehensive because you are not sure you are up to the job (beliefs)? Are you confident that you have the qualification ands skills to make a start (capabilities)? Perhaps you have already 'acted' as a manager, and so have already experienced some of the behaviours you need. Will you be relocated into a manager's office or still in the open plan? How are you affected at the environment level?

Here is an opportunity to make sure you can use all the resources you already have.

Anchors

Now that you have an idea of what changes you can make and what is working well, I should like to suggest that you anchor some of your resources and know that they are there whenever you need them. In NLP terms, an anchor is any stimulus that evokes a consistent response. These can be practical (e.g. the sound of a company fire alarm, which means stop what you are doing and move outside), or emotional (e.g. a photograph of a loved one which makes you feel happy and valued). The power of anchors is based on our ability to learn by making links and forming associations. Once established, they become automatic responses which can be beneficial or detrimental to you. The beneficial anchors are those that trigger resourceful states, like confidence, energy and creativity. The detrimental anchors activate unresourceful states, like depression or frustration and lethargy.

For example: you have had a stressful day at work. You get into your car or onto the bus or train and put on your 'soothing' music tape or take a favourite route. This will calm you down, possibly slow you down and alter your stressed state into a more congenial one. You will be ready for whatever is your next destination. On the other hand, you could get into your car, bus or train, and go over in fine detail all the elements of the meeting that stressed you. You might sit down with a thud, grip the steering wheel tightly, or clutch your briefcase or newspaper tightly, and glare at anyone who considers sitting near you. This will keep you fired up, and speeded up. I wouldn't want to be the next person to meet you!

> Anchoring is the process of connecting a trigger – visual, auditory or kinaesthetic – with a resourceful state, so the response can be quickly re-accessed. An anchor is any cue which will evoke a particular state in an individual.

What works for you?

If you have been nervous or apprehensive about your new role as team leader, you can now choose resourceful anchors to give you the boost you need. If you believe that we all have all the resources we need, then you can transfer what you do well and how you have coped with changes in the past into the team leader role. You may feel you were highly creative when changing the décor at home. Now you can take that creativity into team meetings, coaching, report writing or any other tasks you are taking on.

How you would like to be more resourceful? Decide which resource(s) you need to become a more effective or less nervous team leader. These could include: confidence, calm, energy, concentration, humour or any other resource you choose.

Locate the resource

Think about a time in the past when you have fully experienced that resource you wish to draw upon. It doesn't matter how long ago or whether it was in your professional or personal life. Relive the experience now, seeing the people and things around you as you did at the time. Hear the sounds again, the voices, other noises or maybe the silence. Savour the positive feelings which accompany the experience. Make sure that you are fully associated and experiencing the situation as if you were back in it, not an outside observer. As you recall the resourceful time you may notice physiological changes, too, which indicate a sense of well-being. Enjoy being in your chosen state.

Choose your anchor(s)

You may prefer a visual anchor, such as a particular scene, person or object. An auditory anchor would include sounds, music or voices. A kinaesthetic anchor could involve a gesture to recreate the emotions, sensations and feelings. To create a very powerful trigger you may choose to have all three available. You may see a riverside scene, hear the word 'relax' and squeeze your fingers together to switch yourself instantly into the resourceful state you want.

A successful hockey player described seeing herself on the winners' podium, saying to herself 'yes' and holding her stick upside down before play began as her way of anchoring a resilient and competitive state.

Decide what your anchor will look like, sound like or feel like. Make it different from your regular behaviour so that you do not confuse it with other states and resources. Also choose something discreet that no-one else will notice.

Putting them together

Return to the resourceful time in the past. Re-experience it again and connect with being there. When the feeling is strong and reaching its peak then implement your anchors. Hold them for a few moments and then release them. Shake yourself or move in some way to bring yourself back to the present.

Test it

Remember the initial situation in which you wanted to be more resourceful? Imagine yourself experiencing it now and, as you do so, fire your anchors when they will be most useful as you go through the situation. How did you react? Has your thinking about the original situation changed? Notice you can now switch to a more resourceful state instantly. Anchoring is a skill which needs practice. It becomes easier and more effective the more you use it. Notice those that already work for you and aim to increase them. Notice how you anchor unresourceful states like bad moods and debilitating anxiety. Change the anchors and observe what happens. With resource anchoring you can increase your emotional choice.

What kind of anchor are you?

Are you the type of person others are always pleased to see or do they try to get away if they know you are around? In work situations, take care not to be associated only with bad news or negative feedback and find out how you influence your team. The more you operate from resourceful states, the better company you will be and the more likely you are to be listened to. If you give a balance of feedback when things go well and when they could be better, you will be a well-regarded manager.

A recent description of an England football team manager makes interesting reading:

'... in my experience, teams mimic their managers and the England head coach cuts a gloomy figure on the touchline. When there is always a camera trained on the manager, everyone can see the private, innermost emotions revealed by his body language ... As we see him gritting his teeth and wrinkling his mouth, he seems like a man who doesn't know where he is going – and the team play like that, uncertain and lacking conviction ... The coach needs to transform their body language by changing his.' Tony Cascarino, The Times, 9 February 2007.

Conclusion

Listen to the words your staff use when they are stuck or want your help. Which of the logical levels is at the source? Where can you help them change? Use the core questions and notice what happens. At whichever level you start make sure to ascertain how they align or fit together.

Connectedness / purpose   What is your purpose or the impact you wish to have?

Identity / mission Who are you or what role do you play? Is it the role necessary to achieve your purpose? What do you need to change?

Beliefs / values What beliefs do you have about yourself, about others, about the world in general? Do these beliefs support you in your identity? What do you value – in yourself, in others, and in the world in general? Are these values in alignment with your role? Are there other beliefs and values that you could take on that would be more in alignment?

Capabilities What capabilities do you have? Do you need to develop new skills? Are they in alignment with each of the above logical levels? If not, what needs to be changed? Maybe you need to change your capabilities (get more training). Perhaps, given this new information, you need to reassess your purpose, your role or your beliefs and values

Behaviour What beliefs do you have about yourself, about others, about the world in general? Do these beliefs support you in your identity? What do you value – in yourself, in others, the world in general. Are these values in alignment with your role? Are there other beliefs and values that you could take on that would be more in alignment?

Environment When, where, with whom do you do these behaviours? Are they in alignment with the logical levels above? Where am I doing it?

INSTANT TIP

If change is challenging, check which logical level is most affected.

06

How can I motivate my team?

One of the best ways to motivate your team is to recognise and understand how they motivate themselves. Do some of them look forward to the finishing line in a project whilst others just don't want to be left behind? Do some of them prefer to check what is wanted through consultation with a number of colleagues unlike those who just seem to know what is required and get on with it? You are almost bound to have a number of people in your team who process the information they receive in different ways. Those who are the same as you will seem much easier to motivate and those who are not will, on some occasions, come across as plain awkward. The key here is to recognise that we each have our own way of filtering and sorting the information around us; none is inherently right or wrong, it is simply the way we do it. In NLP, these filters are called metaprograms. When you recognise which filters are being used, you can adjust your communications to fit in with them.

The reason for identifying someone's metaprogram is to appreciate and understand their filters. Once recognised you can work with them from a position of rapport rather than conflict. The implications at work are immense – they can help you fit yourself and others to the jobs which best suit and in which you will be

> Metaprograms are the unconscious filters we use to sort the information we receive in a systematic way which then determines our behaviours. They are systematic and habitual patterns which programme our behaviour at a level of influence that is over and above (meta) everything else. They are determinants of motivation.

most motivated. They can also help you notice how a mismatch between someone's job description and their metaprograms can cause conflict, poor performance and stress-related absences. When you can access someone else's metaprograms, you can give them information using their patterns and they will be able to accept it more easily. When you identify your staff's metaprograms you can adapt your interaction to compensate. You may find you understand them better too. You will be able to work out how best to interact with your team members to find out which jobs suit them best and how to encourage them to fulfil those jobs even better than they do now.

There are numerous metaprograms defined in NLP literature and I am going to outline ten of them that are particularly relevant to you and your team. Each is revealed by asking a question which will indicate the metaprogram being used. A word of warning – metaprograms are contextual. Resist the temptation to label or stereotype when using them.

For example, in a work context I tend to think in terms of the 'big picture' – of course I can write a book on NLP and here are some chapter outlines – that's the easy part. More of a challenge is filling the details for each chapter and putting meat on the bones of the structure. My filters are quite different when I am performing in a show – I become focused on the smallest details. Once I was playing a challenging character which needed a lot of detail and input from the director before I felt I could play it properly. At the technical rehearsal we were organising final positions, lighting, costumes etc. and I was asking whether or not my character would wear nail varnish and if so, what colour! Hardly crucial to the plot, but I couldn't perform without that information.

Motivational direction filter (move towards or away from)

Questions to help uncover this metaprogram:

- What do you want in a job?
- What appeals to you in this project?

The answers to these questions will tell you whether your respondent is motivated towards what they want from their job or project or whether they are more concerned with moving away from an existing or anticipated unpleasant experience. A 'towards' person talks about benefits and knows what they want. They might want job satisfaction, peace of mind at the end of the day, a promotion to aim for or acceptable rewards for a job well done. An 'away from' person talks about problems and is more focused on what to avoid than what to aim for. They might want to avoid working alone, being put under pressure, losing their job or being left out of decision-making. Your 'move towards' team member is likely to be a risk taker with a 'go for it' approach. They may need a 'move away' person to 'reality check' and anticipate possible pitfalls. Your 'move away' person will put off doing something until the last minute, or until the disadvantages of not doing it become great enough to spur them on. Sometimes they respond better to threats than to rewards. They may need a 'towards' person to give them a push start.

Jan and Leigh decided to branch out on their own. I asked them both what they wanted from their new jobs. Jan was keen to be his own boss, have more say about doing the jobs he wanted to do without having to jump through numerous hoops to get approval. A mainly towards motivation with a little away from. Leigh, on the other hand, didn't want to travel as much as at present, didn't want a lot of pressure, and she wanted the opportunity to create a fun-based work environment. Hers was a mainly away from motivation with a little towards.

If I were managing Jan, it would make sense to talk to him about flexibility and choice without too much red tape. In Leigh's case, I would focus on there being no need to work outside the office, that hers was not a stressful post and it provided the chance for her to use her inventiveness.

Reason filter (options – procedures)

Questions to help determine this metaprogram:

- Why are you choosing to do what you are doing?
- Why did you choose your last job?

Options people would give reasons for their choice like, 'the terms and conditions suited me', 'they gave me scope to develop my own style'. They can always think of lots of alternatives and suggest new or better ways to do something. They are motivated in a setting where they have freedom of choice to expand the possibilities available to them. A procedures person would more likely describe *how* they chose, for example: 'I bought all the relevant trade journals, selected vacancies in the areas I would like to move to ...', thus giving you the procedure they followed. They are happy to rely on a system that's already in place, or go through the manual step by step. The procedures person likes to follow the set task sequence and enjoys doing things to meet the 'standard'. They like a clearly defined course of action and detailed instructions.

If someone in your team has an options pattern, they will create variety and choice, but they will want to keep their options open for as long as possible, which can lead to procrastination and unfinished initiatives. I enjoy researching all aspects of a subject and writing the main content of a book. When it comes to topping and tailing or editing a draft, I am much less interested because that is not the time for new ideas. Your procedures-driven team member will want to make sure things go according to plan and run to time. Too many options will create stress and they will search for or make their own procedure. When I am driving somewhere for the first time, I like to have clear instructions from my start to my finish point and I follow them in a very linear way. I note down each motorway exit number and count down from the start to finish. I don't want to know that there are three possible routes to choose from. I want my one set of directions. Without them, I am literally, and metaphorically, lost.

If you or a team member seem to be at one end of the options or procedures continuum, you need to develop some flexibility, because no job will be completely suited to one or the other. Every job needs some development or new ideas whilst having some elements that need to be done in a certain way. An airline pilot will primarily follow procedures but need to be able to handle different options or possibilities if the need arises. An actor will want options and choice in the parts they take, but, while they are acting, will have to follow the procedures in the play.

Relationship filter (sameness – difference)

Questions to help determine this metaprogram:

- How does this job compare with a previous job?
- What is the relationship between the work you are doing now and the work you did last year?

The answer to this question gives you an indication of whether a person sorts information to match for similarities and familiarity – 'still looking at' ... ' the same as before'. Or to mismatch for differences and exceptions – 'changed projects', 'new clients with a different slant', 'the only one that can ...'. A new member of staff who has a matching filter will tell you about the similarities between this and their previous employment. A mismatcher will delight in the differences – to them, a new job is like 'a breath of fresh air'.

A person who prefers to match will probably be happy to stay in the same or similar type of job and not look for changes. They will want a job with stability and a reliable group of people around them. They can often find areas of mutual agreement and can be good mediators. I was running performance management training throughout a large company. It called the course 'career development and staff appraisal'. One of the supervisors on the course seemed very resistant and unprepared to participate. When we talked at the first break she told me she did not want her career to be developed and she was not intending to change what she did. She had been in the same job for 15 years and she liked it. Once reassured that this training was to formalise what she did already, she was able to relax and join in.

If you want your sameness team member to change something, ask them to try out the change for an agreed time and agree, genuinely, if they are not happy after the trial run, what you can change back. It is likely that, once they have experienced the change for a short while and with the insurance of a return, they will stick to what is now the norm and be happy with it.

A mismatcher notices how things are different. They like change and if it isn't forthcoming in their present job, they will make a number of career changes. They are constantly reorganising things, from their desk to the whole department. They may seem to focus on detail. They want to stand out and shine in whatever job they do. A colleague used to dread taking reports to her manager for checking. His first response was to notice the errors and spelling mistakes and only then to tell her how good it was. She wanted him to notice what was good about it *first*, and then she would be able to accept his feedback.

If you have a team member who is a mismatcher and you want them do something it is a good idea to ask 'would you like to work on this project, *or not*?'. The 'or not' will appeal to their need for distinction.

The majority of the population is placed somewhere in between matchers and mismatchers on the relationship filter continuum. Their primary attention is directed towards how things are the same, with a secondary emphasis on the differences. They like jobs which evolve over time and will adapt to changes, as long as they don't occur too often. You can tell when someone is using this filter, as they tend to use comparatives like 'more', 'less', 'better', 'except'. They form a large enough proportion of the population to be the main target for many advertisers. They will reject 'new' unless it is an improved version of the existing model or 'improved' unless it still has some of the original qualities. What could be better than the familiar with some extra spice?

Another large group are those who sort first for difference and then for similarity. People within this pattern will tend to change routines regularly and look for variations of tasks within the overall job they have. So, for example, a nurse specialising in gynaecology will be dealing with different patients but will always be working with babies and their parents.

Frame of reference filter (internal – external)

Questions to help determine this metaprogram:

- How do you know how you're doing in your career?
- How do you know when you're doing a good job?

This is called the 'frame of reference' filter because it refers to the way people form opinions about information they receive and assess their success or otherwise. An externally referenced person will know they are doing a good job when others tell them, or when they hear applause, feel the warmth of approval or see a certificate with a pass mark on it. They like to check out that they are on the right track and will often ask lots of people's opinions before stating their own. They will make their decisions based on the guidance received from others. They are motivated by a conscious awareness of what people want. They respond well to positive feedback regularly given. They can feel demotivated if criticised and completely phased when presented with conflicting calls to action.

An internally referenced person would be likely to answer the above question with words like, 'I just know' or 'I feel good inside'. Internals are self-motivating people who want to make their own decisions. They work best with minimal supervision which recognises their preference to think for themselves. They use their inner feelings as their main way of evaluating success. They do not like close management. To communicate with internals, start by asking for their opinion and avoid telling them what others think. They may well gather information from other people before they make the final decision from their own internal procedures. If you suggest to an internally referenced person that they have a problem, they may respond: 'Yes and the problem is you.' Your externally referenced colleague will think there is something wrong with them and try to put things right between you.

Which of the above filters best describes you? If you are externally referenced you are likely to be concerned about harmony and consensus amongst your team. You want to make sure that everyone has a chance to put across their opinions and share feedback. If you give lots of feedback and encouragement to an internally referenced team member, they may think you are being interfering and disruptive. You need to give them their space to draw their own conclusions – they will want more autonomy and less supervision than you perhaps realised. If you are internally referenced, you may lose rapport with your externals by not giving them enough praise and acknowledgment – after all, you don't need it so why should they? They need to know what you are thinking and that you support them. Left alone for too long, they will become insecure and inefficient.

When I am speaking on a public platform about NLP and how we filter information, I often tell my audience that I am on the externally referenced side of this filter. I then go on to emphasise that I need lots of applause, preferably with them standing, in order to know that I have done a good job. I was recently advised to reconsider plans to have a go at stand-up comedy until I had developed more of an internal reference filter and could asses how well I had done from an internal perspective rather than depending on hysterical laughter from my audience.

Convincer filter 1 (evidence)

Questions to help determine this metaprogram:

- How do you know when someone else is good at what they do?
- How do you convince yourself that someone is competent in their job?

Your replies to this question indicate the sort of evidence you need to be convinced that someone is capable of doing their job. This is useful information for you and your team. Once you have identified your convincer patterns you can suggest ways that team members might present to you in a way that is going to be most acceptable to you. It is also worth considering how your boss is convinced and if their pattern differs from yours, perhaps you can decide how to make changes. The aim here, as with all the metaprograms, is to extend your repertoire and give yourself the best possible chance in your communications.

Do you need:

- To **see** the work they have done, or watch them perform a particular task?
- To **hear** someone tell you they can do it, or hear the evidence, ask colleagues' opinions?
- To **read** reports, testimonials and references, you're convinced if you read about their capability?
- **Hands on experience** with them, or have them perform some sort of trial?

Convincer filter 2 (repetition)

Question to help determine this metaprogram:

- How often does someone have to demonstrate competence before you are convinced?

If you need consistent evidence to convince you that you or someone else is competent in a certain area or with a certain task, you will recognise that this is a difficult pattern to satisfy. This is often the case in the sporting world, where someone is judged as being only as good as their last performance and has to prove themselves again and again. There may be a member of your team who needs to be told about something a number of times or needs a number of different pieces of evidence before they are ready to take on a new task. Or you may have someone who is convinced straight away, automatically assuming the best unless proven otherwise.

A friend was trying to get her daughter to bed. It was getting late and the struggle was escalating. Exasperated, my friend shouted: 'How many times do I have to tell you to go to bed?' 'Four' came the stark reply. This was a young lady who knew her repetition pattern in the going to bed context.

Repetition patterns:

- **A number of times** – You are convinced after a number occasions. Do you know how many it is for you? You might need to see a number of pieces of evidence to have conviction.
- **Over time** – You need to asses someone over a few days, a week, months or years.
- **Automatic** – You accept immediately and give others the benefit of the doubt. You assume they are competent.
- **Consistent** – You are never convinced, proof has to be presented every time. What happens today, may be different tomorrow.

Chunk size filter (general, detail)

Questions to help determine this metaprogram:

- If we were going to work on a project together, would you want to know the big picture, or the details first?
- How did your last project go?

I presented a keynote speech to the marketing arm of a large communications company. They were launching a new product and wanted staff and management to familiarise themselves with it and create a strong team identity with it. Bert, on the front row, seemed to question all the activities I was asking them to engage in. I was not precise enough in my instructions. Of course, he was right – I was not precise enough for *him*. Others were able to get the gist and carry on happily. When I asked Bert what his role was in the company, I was not surprised when he answered 'Financial Director'. I turned to the MD and suggested that they should be delighted Bert was asking all these questions and wanting exact information from me. His detailed approach to his job was what kept them solvent, in profit and in employment. Woe betide them if they have a financial director who is not bothered about the odd hundred pounds here or there.

A 'general' person would cause Bert grief because they think about the big picture and overall concepts. They will often leave out the 'small print' and encourage you to 'get to the point'. They are good at strategic planning and are more interested in total concepts than sequences, steps and stages. If Bert could recognise their challenge with detail and provide summary figures, he might get a better response.

Take a look at the picture opposite. What was the first thing you noticed about it? Look again and see what you missed first time.

'Detail' people first notice the specifics, whilst 'generals' first notice the overview.

The detail person likes to deal with small chunks of data and works well with 'step-by-step' information. They often assess a situation in terms of all the pieces that make up the whole. They may use words like 'precisely' and 'exactly' to make sure everything is as exact as possible. They like to receive information that is broken down into manageable pieces.

We manage information at different levels and in different sized chunks. You can change the way someone is thinking about an issue by 'chunking up' – taking a broader, more general perspective, or 'chunking down' into more detail – discussing a set of tasks necessary for the success of a key project, or 'chunking sideways' – into a related or comparative area of research. 'Helicopter vision' enables you to take a long-term or overview of a project from on high, at the general level. As you chunk down, closer to the ground, you can fill in the details that will lead to its completion.

As a manager you need to be able to chunk down high-level projects and purpose into specific, manageable and delegated tasks. You will also have to chunk up the collective goals of their individual staff to form team and departmental plans. The concept of diversification represents sideways chunking.

Figure 6.1: Adapted from *What Makes People Tick?* By Susan Quilliam

Action filter (proactive, reactive)

Questions to help determine this metaprogram:

● How do you 'take the initiative?'
● Do you act quickly in a new situation, or wait and study the consequences first?

Proactive people take the initiative by getting on with things at their own prompting. They are self-starters who shoot first and ask questions later. Reactive people wait and respond to others who ask for help. They are good at analysing tasks and gathering information before taking action. Proactive people can make mistakes by ignoring the analysis and planning stages in decision-making. Reactive people may slow things down by too much analysis or because they are waiting for someone else to take responsibility.

If a customer complains to a proactive member of staff, they can expect something to be done immediately. It may not be exactly what they need, but there will be speedy response. A reactive staff member would take lengthy notes and pass them on to a supervisor. Understanding the customer's metaprogram will determine which style they prefer and strengthen the relationship.

Primary interest filter (people and places)

Think about the best holiday you ever had. The elements you remember will depend on the filters you use. Knowing that none is right or wrong, recognise the way you sort information.

Holiday memories might focus on:

- **People** – those you went with, the charm of the locals, the tour guides, new friends.
- **Places** – the location, beaches, restaurants, airports, your favourite bar.
- **Things** – mementos, gifts, local produce, video / photos, silly sun hat.
- **Activity** – a tour of the island, theme nights, snorkelling, sunbathing.
- **Time** – when it happened, dates, what you did day by day.

At work it is very useful to recognise another person's focus of interest in a particular context. Being *people focused* is important for staff at the customer interface as they will respond better to the customer's needs. An *activity focus* will be helpful to someone who is organising the weekly rotas.

Which focus is important in your job? Which is your favourite?

Time storage (in or through time)

The way we relate to time also has implications for the way we communicate. Some people seem to live in the past, remembering the way things were. They might talk about how things were done in their last job. Others live for now and their attention is on the present moment. They talk about the here and now: let's do it. Future-oriented people tend to plan and be thinking about the future – the sort of person who wants to know what they will be having for tea just as they finish their lunch. Consider which way you relate to time and those around you. What could you change to take you closer to them? There are benefits to any team if you have all three available, as long as they appreciate each other's value to the team.

Timelines

People code time in different ways. We may use the same words, past, present, future, but we will place them differently in the way we represent them in our minds. How do you know whether something is a past memory or a plan for the future? In NLP, the term 'timeline' is used to explain where people position their concepts of time.

Find your timeline:

- Think about four events from your past which cover your life to date.
  Where were those memories positioned? If you were to point to their location, would they be behind, in front, to the left or to the right of you?
- As you read this book now, decide where 'now' is.
  Point to indicate: is it inside you, in front of you, or to the left or right of you?
- Now think about three probable events from your future, starting with next week and going as far ahead as you wish.
  Where were those thoughts positioned? Point to their location and notice from which direction they came.

This will give you an idea of where you place time and, if you were to plot and join up the dots, you could trace the direction of your line.

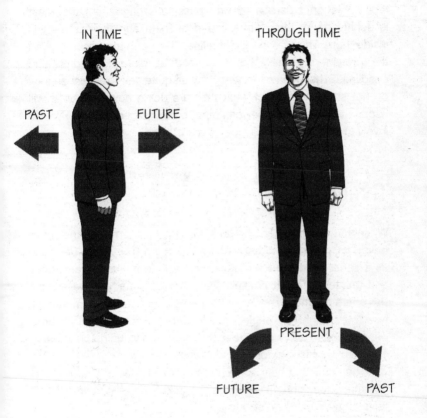

Figure 6.2: Through time and in time timelines

In time

The timeline known as 'in time' is so called because, in this representation, a person has time passing through them, their past is behind them, their future ahead of them and their present is inside them. They are in their timeline. They tend to concentrate on the present and may be less good at planning and setting deadlines. Their idea of 'urgent' may be quite flexible because they do not strongly connect what they are doing now with what will happen in the future. They can tend to be late because they are so involved in now and easily lose track of time.

Through time

When someone is operating on a 'through time' timeline, they have their past, present and future in front of them. They think of events as a series of related episodes, where time is linear, continuous and uninterrupted. It is likely that 'through time' people are the designers of time management schemes, and cannot comprehend how they might be unclear to 'in time' people. 'Through time' people tend to arrive on time and place a high value on punctuality. They are excellent at forward planning.

When you next hear someone say, 'I can't see any future ...' or 'the future looks bright', they may be talking more literally than you would have thought previously.

Warning

Time lines and metaprograms give an overview of how people process information and their resultant behaviour. They are not a way to label people, because they change in different contexts, they are descriptions of behaviour. In many cases, you and your staff will have a combination of the metaprograms with, occasionally, someone being at one extreme of the continuum. As with all NLP concepts, their purpose is to enable you to think about patterns that help you understand and communicate better. You can use your rapport to match language and behaviour, or perceptual positions to discover how a situation seems from someone else's world.

Conclusion

Enjoy discovering which metaprograms best describe your preferences. They can explain so much about communications and help you understand when team members are working from different ones.

- Which metaprograms do you prefer at work? Where are they most / least effective?
- Are there some tasks you prefer not to do? Can this be explained through your metaprograms?
- Imagine a previous project, how might it have been handled to accommodate different people's metaprograms What does this tell you for the future?

In the following table, the language column briefly describes the words they might use and the response column suggests additional words you might use to establish rapport.

Metaprograms	Language they use	work pattern / role	your response
towards	get, have, gain, attain, accomplish	sales, innovation, inventor, designer	goal-oriented, hope for incentives
away from	avoid, steer clear, exclude, prevent	problem solving, health and safety	point out dangers of not doing, exclude
match	usual, familiar, in common	mediation, trends negotiation	same as, traditional
mismatch	new, change, one-off, different	marketing, consultancy	unique, special, revolutionary
internal reference	I decide, I made the decision ...	web design, writer performer, lawyer	only you can decide, only you will know

external reference	what do you think? is that OK?	PA bank teller, travel agent, civil servant	others think, the facts show
general	overall, big picture, globally, flexible	explorer, policy-maker, strategy	basically, framework overview, roughly
detail	specifically, precisely, schedule	pilot, architect, finance, editor	structure, exactly, let's be clear
options	choice, possibility	teachers	alternatives, options
procedure	needed to, must	filing, accounts	known way, proven
proactive	initiative, action, future plans	fundraiser, journalist, sales, entrepreneur	independent, direct
reactive	respond, reaction, past achievement	help desk, call centre, receptionist	analysis, waiting

INSTANT TIP

Try out opposite metaprograms to understand your staff better – eg, if you prefer detail, try considering the big picture and vice versa.

07

How can I use NLP in my coaching?

The phenomenon of coaching has exploded in the business world in recent years. It was always the norm and necessity to have coaches in the performing and sporting arenas; now they proliferate everywhere. You will be expected to coach your team in your role as team leader and NLP is a great asset to help you do so. If you think about it, you will realise that coaching is happening all the time, both *by* you and *to* you. Coaching is the art of improving the performance of others. Regular coaching will help you and your team to do your jobs more effectively. It happens when you help someone bridge a gap in their performance or when you want to highlight and encourage their best practice. As a manager, you can encourage your team and the individuals within it to learn from, be motivated and be challenged by their work. You can create the conditions for continuous development in a seemingly informal way – it can occur in the corridor, or after a meeting, on the way to an event. You have an endless choice of coaching opportunities any time you are talking to your team. In this chapter I will be considering coaching as a spontaneous activity – a leadership style that happens naturally, and once you have practised the techniques that follow, that is exactly what it will be. It will become part of your unconscious programming, just like eating and drinking are now.

Adam Cox, associate director of Radio Relations suggests that:

'A coach doesn't necessarily need to be able to actually do the things they are coaching but they need to have the knowledge of the practical distinctions that can make the biggest difference in outcome. A key aspect of NLP is to model belief systems, physiology and behaviour to be able to achieve the right outcome consistently. A coach has the experience and ability to communicate those distinctions in a way that can be replicated by the team consistently.

For example, when I am coaching new sales people, part of their process is to speak to senior marketing decision-makers whom they have never spoken to before (also known as cold calling). The habitual pattern of most new sales people is to ask to speak directly to the head of marketing. Secretaries and receptionists are often briefed not to transfer sales people, they take the role of 'gatekeeper' and will never put the call through. A simple distinction is always to introduce yourself and treat the receptionist as a signpost rather than a gatekeeper. By asking the name of the head of marketing, rather than to be put straight through, you will often get the name immediately. If the sales person simply asks "is [first name] available?", they will generally get straight through to the person they want to speak to, rather than being screened out. This is a simple distinction but makes a massive difference in the outcome between those who apply the distinction and those who do not. The role of a coach is to know how to articulate the right distinction at the right time depending on the needs of the team member.'

An NLP lynchpin, behavioural flexibility, has been implicitly present throughout this book. It has an explicit place in most coaching scenarios. If your coachee's actions are not achieving the results they want, then your job is to help them do something else. Seems obvious, doesn't it? Yet so many of us keep on doing the same thing, convinced it will eventually lead to the desired outcome. Have you ever looked for a report or a book that you know you have and just not been able to find it? If you are anything like me, you can repeat the searching sequence even though it didn't work first time, become increasingly frustrated and get nowhere fast. When I am exercising my behavioural flexibility, I leave the room, change state, and assure myself it will turn up soon enough. And more often than not it does! It is all encapsulated in that well-known NLP phrase:

'If what you're doing isn't working, try something – anything else.'

There is a parallel process between your confidence and competence with NLP and the skills and confidence you want to instil with your coaching. There are a number of stages associated with learning any new skill and the competency cycle is a very useful way of tracking them. Let us take the example of my learning to be an NLP practitioner. Before I started my training, I had heard of NLP and thought it was probably cognitively based and similar to the counselling training I had undertaken. I was in the stage of *unconscious incompetence* – I didn't know what I didn't know about NLP. I was unaware of the many tools and techniques it offered and I knew nothing about the founders and their processes of creating it. I went along to my training in a state of curiosity and anticipation. I love to learn about myself and how to transfer that learning to others. Once we started the training, I entered the stage of *conscious incompetence*: I began to realise just how much I didn't know about NLP. It had so many terms I had not previously encountered and so many techniques, like anchoring, the meta model and calibration, that I did not think I would ever be able to manage them all. I was suddenly aware of trying things out and getting them wrong. Happily, I soon moved into the *conscious competence* stage of my NLP training. I was aware of when things were going right. I was able to take someone through a perceptual positions exercise and we both experienced the level of insight and information they gained about what had appeared to be an insurmountable relationship problem for them at work. I was able to use my training to select a resourceful technique and consciously take my coachee through each position to enable their growth. I felt great and was delighted with my progress. Nowadays, there are times when I am in *unconscious competence* in my use of NLP. This was highlighted when I wrote my last book.

When I was asked to write *Shift Your Thinking, Change Your Life*, I was briefed that it was to be a personal development book based around the ideas and coaching articles that I was writing for a health and beauty magazine. Each month I was taking a reader and her issues as a case study, giving her a telephone consultation and then writing the results up in a generalised way, so as to be helpful to as many readers as possible. Once the book was written, I was wanted to promote it and was offered various opportunities to do so in my capacity as a professional speaker. When a branch of the Chartered Institute for Marketing asked me to combine 'Shift Your Thinking' with an NLP approach to communications, I was surprised at how easy this was. I hadn't realised how much NLP had become a part of my thinking and processing. I had written the book with a covert NLP influence.

In Figure 7.1, the arrows are pointing in both directions for two reasons. First, you are now ready for new learnings and, secondly, it is worth checking occasionally that your habit is still working in a resourceful way. We can slip into unconscious incompetence without realising. Think about the stages of learning to drive a car. I would guess that if you are a car driver you may have developed a few bad habits that you weren't even aware of. (Until now, of course, as I have just brought them into your awareness.)

This model is very useful to consider when you are going to

make a coaching intervention with one of your team. It is worthwhile finding out where your coachee is on the competence model, rather than assuming they know what they could be doing, just because you do. A key part of coaching is to help the other person believe for themselves in their own brilliance and your role is to help them find it.

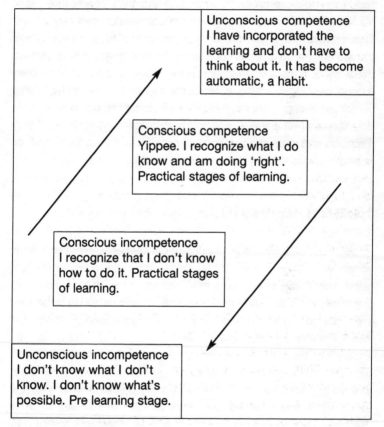

Unconscious competence
I have incorporated the learning and don't have to think about it. It has become automatic, a habit.

Conscious competence
Yippee. I recognize what I do know and am doing 'right'. Practical stages of learning.

Conscious incompetence
I recognize that I don't know how to do it. Practical stages of learning.

Unconscious incompetence
I don't know what I don't know. I don't know what's possible. Pre learning stage.

Figure 7.1: The competency cycle

When a team member gets to the stage of unconscious competence, they can effectively perform their task on auto pilot. This is great when they are performing their work in the best possible way. Sometimes, when your staff are working on auto pilot, they achieve poor results, because their way of working is not correct. The role of a coach in this context is to break down the task back to its original components and then ensure the team member 're-learns' the task, going through the competency model. This is when it is important for you, as coach, to be aware of the competency model, since your team member may get frustrated at the point of conscious incompetence. They have effectively taken a step back from being able to do something without thinking (albeit the wrong way), to doing the right thing but doing it badly. It is important to pace this experience and reassure the team member that conscious incompetence is just a natural part of relearning how to carry out a task in the right way.

Learning styles

Another set of information to consider is that of learning styles. In which ways do you and your team members like to learn? Do you learn how to use a new piece of equipment through trial and error, switching it on and experimenting until it seems to do what you want? Or do you like to go through the manual working through the examples step by step until you feel proficient? Neither is right or wrong and they can lead to misunderstanding and resentment if they are not respected in any learning situation. Know your style and be prepared to put your preference to one side when you are focusing on the coachee and want to help them learn in their preferred style. Be prepared to accept their approach and, if it is different from yours, you may learn something too. The learning styles outlined below are generally ascribed to Honey and Mumford.

- **Activists** These learners involve themselves fully in new experiences and like to be involved in activity. They relish coping with crises, are optimistic about anything new and are unlikely to resist change. Once the initial excitement is over, they tend to get bored with implementation and consolidation. They enjoy working with others but tend to do too much themselves and hog the limelight. They are likely to say: 'I often act without considering the possible consequences', 'I actively seek new experiences.'

- **Reflectors** Reflectors like to collect all the facts and to look at situations from all the angles. They are careful and methodical and dislike reaching a conclusion until they have thought it through thoroughly. They prefer to take a back seat, observing and listening to others but often tend to be too cautious and not take enough risks. They are likely to say: 'I like time to prepare thoroughly', 'I'm always interested to find out what others think.'

- **Theorists** Theorists approach situations logically, working through step by step, integrating their observations into complex theories. They tend to be perfectionists and reject ideas they see as subjective or intuitive. Their disciplined approach restricts their ability to think creatively and they are unlikely to be prepared to give it a go and see what happens. They are likely to say: 'I am often the most dispassionate and objective person in a discussion.'

- **Pragmatists** Pragmatists are practical, businesslike individuals who like to get straight to the point. They are full of ideas and keen to try them out straight away. They are most comfortable with things that they know are going to work and tend to reject ideas without an obvious application. They are impatient with what they see as 'waffle'. If you are a pragmatist, beware of a tendency to seize on the first expedient solution to a problem. They are likely to say: 'What matters most is whether something works in practice.'

It is worth revisiting representational systems in Chapter 4, to check their impact on learning too. You will be able to create great rapport with your coachees when you can match their learning styles and representational systems. They will be far more amenable to learning and changing if they believe you understand their map of the world.

The visuals learn through seeing. Equip yourself with pictures, diagrams, demonstrations, reading or a DVD for them to watch.

Your auditory team members learn through hearing. Equip yourself with audio CDs or downloads, lectures, discussions and verbal instructions. Be prepared for debates with these people.

Kinaesthetics learn through physical activities and direct involvement. They like to be hands-on, moving, touching, experiencing. Equip yourself with something they can do and be prepared to coach them on the move; they may think better that way, rather than standing in the corridor or sitting at their desk.

Whilst I was doing my research for this book, I spent many hours on the phone talking to colleagues about its structure and contents. My mind clarifies my ideas when I can talk them through. I do not necessarily want any answers or suggestions – I need to hear myself thinking about my ideas before they become print worthy.

Language

In Chapter 4 you had the chance to consider the words you and other people use and decide how they indicate VAK preferences. I want to broaden this out now and invite you to notice the effect your language has on your feelings and behaviours and those of people around you.

Stephanie Holland and David Morton at Rapport Communications Consultancy often refer to 'toxic' language, which can poison our minds and thoughts. Their description and explanation is as follows:

'The language we use both to others and in our thoughts has an amazing effect on the way we motivate ourselves and other people. Every word we have ever heard ourselves and others speak is stored inside our brain in a giant filing system just waiting to be "re-activated" when a similar word or idea is used.

Using negative words such as:

trouble	*problem*	*difficult*
disastrous	*nightmare*	*complaint*

will instantly open similar negative files in either our own mind or the minds of others. For example, a word like "difficult" will be stored in a file full of linked words with similar meaning e.g. *hard, troublesome, awful, hassle.*

If you constantly use phrases such as:
*Could I trouble you? This is going to be hard
I'm sorry to bother you Excuse me – I have a complaint
This has turned into a nightmare It's no problem*

you will be triggering a list of negative ideas and phrases in other people's minds which will put them on the defensive and will stimulate similar negative responses. You will also de-energise yourself, depress your own optimism and set your thoughts in a downward spiral.

Change your negative phrases to positive ones:

problem	becomes	**challenge**
don't forget		**remember**
I've got a complaint		**I'd like your help**
I must		**I choose to**
I need more effort		**I need more energy**
It's not bad		**It's excellent**
I'm ok		**I'm wonderful**

You will really notice the difference when you spring-clean your mind and clear your vocabulary of years worth of negativity. This difference is due to the "mind-body" link, which ensures that a completely different set of chemicals are released into your bloodstream when you use positive words and thoughts compared to when you use negative ones. Positive language means that your body will feel lighter and more energetic, your posture will become more upright and confident and you will give out a different, more attractive aura. Above all, other people's response to you will be more helpful, more co-operative and more positive.'

The implications for this in a coaching conversation are many. Are your team giving themselves the best chance throughout the business with positive and affirming language, or are they setting themselves up for a rough ride as they put themselves down or keep their negative files open? In Chapter 1 I mentioned my colleague's millstone that kept her from writing her thesis. Her negative connotation of what was involved was seriously damaging her success possibilities. Changing her language to talk about her winner's medal helped her progress.

As you become more aware how your thoughts affect you, you can choose whether to hold on to the negative ones and be miserable or change them for ones that are more positive and enabling. The first thing is to notice and think about what you are saying to yourself, what you hear, what you see or how you feel. Awareness means you are conscious of the choices available. This is also very valuable learning for your team members. As you notice their language, you can gently challenge the impact of their words and help them make changes. A simple example is to change a throw-away criticism like 'stop being snappy' to a request that someone 'start behaving calmly and listen to all angles'.

'It's better to light the candle than curse the darkness.' Eleanor Roosevelt

Remember a time when you've worried about doing something you haven't wanted to do, or you've been nervous or anxious about something. How have you prepared yourself? Did you think: 'Well this is one meeting. I can handle it, I know what's going on here'? Or did you think, 'Oh it's going to be awful. It's going to be as bad as it was last time', or 'I don't know how bad it's going to be, but I know its going to be bad', or 'Everybody's told me I can't expect anything from him' or 'She's always going to shout, you know what she's like'? Your language impacts the way you feel, how you prepare and how you act in any situation.

Another case in point is when you consider the question: what do you talk about at the end of a day? How often do you go home from work, or at the end of a project, sit down and you say to anyone who is listening: 'Let me tell you about the best thing that happened to me today', or 'Do you know, there was one really great thing that happened to me today'? If your answer is 'often', that's great. If not, why not? Perhaps you recognise this scene better. You go home and you say: 'You'll never believe the day I had today! I tell you, everything that could have gone wrong went wrong.' Think about the tone of your voice, your feelings and your body language when you say that sort of thing.

If it hasn't been your best ever day, do you want to make sure you have a rotten night too? Do you want to stay in a bad mood and bring everyone else down? Would you prefer to let go and enjoy whatever you can. Start to notice the 'nuggets of gold' that happen to you during your day. The little things that make you smile as well as the great big ones that make you jump for joy. Record them in some way every day. It may seem a bit strange at first. Persevere and you will have a collection that will inspire you. When you record what you are happy with, it stays with you and over time becomes your positive focus, a great place for your unconscious to be. Encourage your staff to do the same and notice the buzz that it creates as people are empowered to share their achievements rather than wallow in their misfortunes.

The Milton model

The Milton model is the inverse of the meta model and both have a place in coaching. The meta model enables you and your coachee to clarify and understand what they are saying and thinking abut the issues they encounter. It engages people in reality testing and is predominantly working with the mind at a conscious level. It was developed from the work of Satir and Perls, who asked questions to help recover deleted information, and reveal distortions and generalisations. On the other hand, Erickson's success often came through telling stories and talking in a way that was vague and ambiguous. Using the Milton model will enable you to develop what Milton Erickson described as 'artfully vague' language, that is deliberately ambiguous and abstract. This means that the listener will have to access resources in their unconscious mind to find their own meaning and way forward. Leaving out information is an important part of the Milton model because that keeps the conscious mind busy filling in the gaps from its store of memories. When your coachee searches for meaning from their own experience, they will be making a meaning that is most relevant and appropriate to them. You don't have to know the answers – you are providing questions or statements that will help them work things out for themselves. Erickson used fuzzy, hypnotic language to challenge people in a subtle, non-threatening way and from their map of the world. He offered no direct suggestions and plenty of scope for their unconscious mind to do the processing it required.

The following hypnotic language patterns are very powerful in coaching, training and other influence situations. They create the same kind of trance that we experience when we are daydreaming or get lost in a book or piece of music. When we are on 'automatic pilot', we are in a trance. It is a naturally occurring state, one we go into and out of regularly throughout a day.

Here are some examples of how Erickson helped people to focus on their internal representations and effect change through their unconscious processing. Experiment with them and notice how they increase your coaching capability.

Complex equivalence
'That means ... the fact that you've asked my advice means that you are ready to find the solutions.'

This is a great way to create a positive framework for your coaching session, where two things – or their meanings – are equated as synonymous.

Mind reading
'I know that you are learning ...'
Claiming to know what the other person is thinking can make your suggestions more acceptable. It can strengthen rapport.

Lost performative
'It's important to experiment with language patterns ...'

Value judgements where the source of the evaluation or judgement is omitted. This can be a good way to bypass resistance

Cause-effect
'Because ... you can start to make those changes because you've waited long enough.'

People like to have reasons to do things and are more likely to respond positively when you imply that one thing leads to another.

Presuppositions
'You have many valuable skills and resources available to you at a moment's notice ... I wonder if you realise how valuable you are to the team?'

These are the linguistic assumptions which lead to unconscious agreement because you presuppose what you don't want to be questioned.

Universal quantifiers
'You can learn from every situation ...'

Words that are absolute generalisations, and so are more credible to the unconscious mind. Key words include: 'any', 'always', 'never', 'every', 'all', 'none' etc.

Modal operators
'You can generate many creative ideas ... you don't have to try, it will sort itself out ...'

Words which dictate or imply what is possible and/or necessary in our life.

Nominalisations
'Insights, understandings and discoveries await you ...'

These are process words that have been frozen by making them into a noun.

Unspecified verbs

'And you can understand ...'

Process words which lack a complete description. Verbs that can work in this way include 'experiences', 'feel', 'sense', 'understand' and 'learn'. They imply action without describing how the action takes place.

Tag questions

'Can't you?'.. It's useful to try out new models, isn't it?'

A question added to the end of a statement which is difficult to disagree with. It will usually create an affirmative answer.

Lack of referential index

'A person can you know' ... 'A person can achieve so much with an open mind ...'

A phrase which deletes who is doing the acting. The unconscious mind has to draw on their own experiences to understand the statement.

Pacing current experience

'As you are sitting here, looking at this book and reading this ...'

Truisms about the listener's current, ongoing sensory experience.

Double binds

'I don't know whether you'll discover just what you've learned ... now, in a few moments from now, or sometime later ...'

Statements or questions, which engage one's attention on a consequence which presupposes something else. It creates what Erickson called 'an illusion of choice'.

There are some additional Milton patterns I want to mention that are not direct meta model violations, and are extremely useful ways of communicating with a person's unconscious.

Quotes enable you to use reported language that give the listener's conscious mind nothing to resist while their unconscious mind will take it as a command, especially when special emphasis is given to the key words.

'In one session, my coach said: *"acknowledge your strengths and build on them"*.'

An embedded command is an instruction, which is interpreted differently by the unconscious and conscious minds. For example, if you say: 'It's good to be in a place where people like to *enjoy new learnings*' and you use a slightly different tone of voice for the words *enjoy new learnings*, then this is what will happen. Your listeners' conscious minds will register the whole sentence, while their unconscious minds will register the instruction *enjoy new learnings* and act accordingly. Every time you say to someone 'Don't *do that*!', you are giving an embedded command. The conscious message is, of course, 'Don't do that'. In order for the brain to process the instruction 'Don't do that', it has to form an image of whatever that is. In so doing, the message to the unconscious brain – the embedded command – is to do it!

That's why if you say to a child who is carefully walking with a full glass of water 'Don't spill the water!', you can practically guarantee that they will. Tell people what you do want them to do – 'Walk carefully'.

Embedded questions do not overtly ask for a response because they use a form of words that seem to be rhetorical. The embedding comes about when you place emphasis on particular parts of the sentence.

> 'I'm wondering whether ...'
> 'I am curious to know ...'
> 'I'm asking myself whether ...'
> 'I'm curious to know what it will be like for you to *take a fresh approach to coaching*.'
> 'I'm wondering if you can *believe how effective you are* at managing customers.'

This model often revives the 'isn't it manipulative?' question – i.e. giving people commands that only their unconscious is aware of. The answer is that, of course, you are addressing the people's unconscious minds all the time. Almost every time you open your mouth you are giving an embedded command – which may not necessarily be very helpful. A coach who says 'Don't *worry about the coaching process*' is certainly sending a powerful and unhelpful message. As you are doing it anyway, isn't it better to *be aware of what you are doing*, so that you can *use it ethically and in the interests of your team*?

Here are some direct questions which can also help your coachee access their unconscious thinking and resources:

> 'What happens when you imagine ...?'
> 'What happens when you imagine being able to do this easily?'
> 'What happens when you imagine feeling good in this situation? What happens when you imagine having put this problem behind you?'

In order to make sense of the question, the person has to imagine doing it. And when you imagine doing something, you are one step closer to doing it for real.

> 'How will you feel when (the issue) is no longer an issue?'
> 'How will you feel when your relationship with senior staff is no longer an issue?'

This question invites your coachee to experience life without the problem. It directs their attention to a place beyond the 'how' of resolving it. If the coachee is willing to stay with that feeling, they will often find the resources to affect their own solution.

> 'If you did know, what would the answer be?'

This is one of my favourite questions. You can use it after your coachee has said 'I don't know'. It is really important to have rapport, otherwise your coachee will get defensive and assume you are not listening.

Conclusion

- Identify some things that you would like your team members to do. Perhaps you want them to take more initiative, appreciate their skills or speak up at meetings.
- What could you get them to imagine that will get them a step closer to doing what you want them to do? Do you want them to imagine taking action unprompted, accepting positive feedback or comfortably standing up and making a point in a meeting?
- Create a question using the 'What happens when you imagine ...?' pattern. What happens when you imagine taking action unprompted? What happens when you imagine accepting positive feedback and believing the good things people say about you? What happens when you imagine comfortably standing up and making a point in a meeting?
- Then get into rapport with the person and ask them the question. Notice and enjoy the results. Your coaching will be a rewarding experience for both you and your coachee as you become more comfortable and proficient with these patterns.

INSTANT TIP

Help your coachees recognise toxic language and change it to enriching language.

08

Will NLP make presentations and meetings any easier?

Let's get the negatives out of the way from the beginning. American research in the 1980s asked people what they most feared. The conclusions were surprising; more people were afraid of walking into a room full of strangers or speaking in public than they were of dying. If this is you, it won't be by the end of this chapter. As far as I'm concerned, speaking is something most of us do naturally all the time and a presentation is just a conversation between you and a number of other people. Even if you are anticipating taking team meetings for the first time or need to represent your team at business meetings, these are still conversations. In Chapter 2 we considered how beliefs drive our behaviour and if you still believe it's not safe to talk to strangers, this is a limiting belief that will affect how you make a presentation or inhibit your success at networking events. The belief impacts on your behaviour. If you believe that public speaking is terrifying, that will be transmitted in your presentation. Your audience will be aware of your underlying discomfort and will focus on that, rather than your message.

I have known people refuse to apply for promotions because it would mean making presentations inside and outside the business and they were not going to set themselves up for that sort of pain.

What are you afraid of? Is it that you will be judged and found wanting? Perhaps you are worried you will be exposed as someone who doesn't know the subject, or are you plain scared that you will make a fool of yourself, 'dry up', stammer, drop all your notes, that others will laugh inappropriately, or that you will blush so extremely that everyone will stare at you? The good news is that any fear you associate with making presentations is a learned response which can be unlearned.

Marcel remembered back to his time at school. He was expected to make speeches in his English class and found this very difficult. As he recalled what was happening, he realised he was thinking about a teacher who would ridicule his accent and have the class join in the joke. Whenever he stood up at a meeting or in a presentation he was unconsciously whisked back to an old, unwanted story that was of no relevance to who he is today. He was unconsciously re-experiencing the state that had held him back for many years and it had become an automatic response. As we unravelled what was happening, we started to change his response to a new, empowering one.

I told Marcel: 'The good news is that your unconscious is demonstrating how smart it is. Having experienced ridicule at school, it has decided to protect you from further danger by putting you on fear alert every time you think about presentations, and it is taking you away from having to endure them. Now, if your unconscious learnt so quickly to fire your fear response, it can easily learn to replace it with a facilitating one. All you have to do is reprogramme yourself, now.'

There were a number of ways I was able to help Marcel, and I will describe them through the rest of this chapter. I don't know which of them will be the most helpful for you or whether you will feel the benefits immediately or in a few weeks when you next present.

So what do you need in order to present confidently to any audience? Preparation of yourself is key to feeling good about presenting. Think about the anchors you created in Chapter 5 – they will be useful here too. Do you need more confidence or calmness when you speak? Find a way to access them now and you will immediately feel more resourceful.

State management

Have you ever heard anyone say that they are in a rotten state? It usually means that they are not in control of what is happening or that they are not in a good place. Someone else might tell you that, in order to succeed in a new task, you need to be in the right state of mind. In NLP terms, a state represents all the thoughts, emotions and physiology that you express in any given moment. It comes from what you are sensing; the pictures, sounds, smells, tastes, what you are feeling; your emotions, what you are thinking; your mental activity, what is happening in your brain; your neurological activity and what is going on in your body; your posture, breathing and your energy levels. You are always in some kind of state, though not always consciously aware of it. Your states will change throughout the day, responding to internal and external circumstances. Sometimes you are aware of them, sometimes not. States intensely affect how you feel and determine how you behave. They can be limiting or empowering and impact on your ability to perform well. When you feel on top of the world, you will tackle anything and act with courage. When you feel down in the dumps, you are more likely to withdraw, do as little as possible and do it with apprehension. Many people really do not know how to describe how they are feeling much of the time, and can feel stuck without realising why. Once you recognise your states, you have the choice to change them.

One of the quickest and easiest ways to change your state of mind is to change your physiology. Get up out of your chair and walk around, dance to some jazzy music, jump up and down, shake your hands, sing out loud or change your breathing. These are all ways to break out of undesired states. By the same token, adopting the postures and stances that you take when you are performing at a high level can bring up those high performance states.

If you accept that most people have an attention span of around 15 minutes, then you can use a variation of the ideas above to change their state and keep them engaged with your presentation. Have them talk to a neighbour for a couple of minutes or have them stand up and find someone new to talk to. I know a presenter who uses musical anchors to change state outrageously. Whenever his audience hears a particular piece of cartoon music, they have to stand up, rub their stomachs and pat their heads while turning around on the spot. This music is apparently played at random intervals, though, of course, it is strategically used when he wants to break the present state and move into another one. At an unconscious level, his audience is ready for the new segment of information that is coming their way.

You can employ musical anchors more conventionally in a number other specific ways. You can create a certain state or mood when your team or audience enter the location of the presentation by playing calming or raucous music, or anything in between. You can also have the key message on PowerPoint or on posters around the room and you can have some sort of object for them to handle and play with – all before the formal presentation begins. Some presenters like to put gentle music on in the background when people are working in small groups as an aid to their thinking. Using one specific piece of music to bring people back to the group when they have been working together or out on a break is much more effective than tapping a glass or trying to shout above the noise they are making. It is kinder on your voice too. One colleague walks into the training room, holds his pen in the air and everyone stops to pay attention to him.

There are two aspects of state management that relate to presentations and meetings. The first is to consider what state you want to be in before you present and right through to the end of your presentation. The second and related one is to know what state you want your audience to be in at any given time. The way you feel and the state you are in will be picked up by your audience, so it's a good idea to decide consciously how you want to be.

If you want your audience to be in a positive learning state, think first about a time when you felt that way so you can access it for yourself, then ask the audience directly to: 'recall a time when you enjoyed learning a new skill'. Or indirectly: 'You know how sometimes you seem to just learn something new without even trying? It's great isn't it?' You don't need to elaborate any more, you have just helped your audience find their positive learning state. You have opened up that part of their brain. The more expressive you are, the more expressiveness you will get from your audience. If your posture, voice tone, words and facial expression match the response you want, you are more likely to get it. If you want your audience to find a calm and resourceful state, but you are talking loudly and quickly, moving around a lot and relying on soothing words, you will be greatly disappointed. They are more likely to become restless. Now give them the learning you want them to have. Create the state you want them to experience and then you can confidently give them the messages or information you want them to retain.

Maintaining an open and confident state is an important factor in giving a presentation. Shoulders slumped, looking down or standing lopsided will stimulate sets of chemicals in your nervous system that will not support you physically or emotionally as a presenter. On the other hand, standing upright, with feet grounded, shoulders relaxed and breathing slowly will send chemicals to the brain that will be much more conducive to confidence. Keep your head up, speak clearly in a confident tone and act as if you are confident (and of course you will then feel confident). When your words, tone and body language are congruent, and all give out the same message, your audience will be ready and able to believe you.

Speak their language

Remember that Chapter 4 considered the different representational systems (VAK) that people use – some like to make pictures in their minds (visuals), some prefer to talk things over to understand (auditory), and others connect information to their feelings and when it feels right it becomes concrete (kinaesthetic). It is essential for your audience in any presentation or meeting, that you provide information in all three styles. For the visuals, talk about the pictures you want to create, how you *see* the business developing and check that it *looks good* to them. The auditories want to know what your development ideas *sound* like – they want to know that you are all singing from the same hymn sheet and they are happy for you to check that it 'rings a bell' for them. You want the kinaesthetics in the audience to *get a handle* on your plans, know that you are *on common ground* and they like you to check their *gut reaction*. It is a good idea to review the words and phrases provided in Chapter 4 and start to build your own collection of predicates and phrase to include all styles in your meetings and presentations.

Another idea is to embed your presentations with a mixture of activities to engage each representational system too. The kinaesthetics in your audience will respond best to working practically, being the 'live demonstration model', moving around and, where possible, being hands on. The auditories might want a CD as back up and the chance to ask questions. They will respond well to the use of music and will notice the voice tones you use. The visuals in your audience will appreciate diagrams, charts and handouts to look at. They want to be hands on as well.

A colleague of mine, Chris Davidson, is an expert in giving people the skills and confidence to perform in public. He gave me the following case study, which is a great example of how to cover VAK in presenting and how to set the session off with a powerful beginning theme. He believes the first 90 seconds of a presentation encapsulates the whole session, so you need to hit the floor running (especially if you are kinaesthetic).

Chris was working with Shula, a polite and well-mannered communications director in the transport industry. She needed to get home the point that, while they were selling seats for £100 that was fine, but once the train had left the station, any empty seat was a £100 loss. Therefore, it made better sense to sell seats at the last minute for £10 to create some income. She knew this wasn't going to be well received and was somewhat timid in her approach. She and Chris played around with a few ideas and then came up with the following.

Shula was to open her presentation with a question (always good to gain attention and much better than 'good morning' or 'it's lovely to be here': people blank out those statements and can lose interest before you've started). She held up a tin of baked beans in one hand and a banana in the other.

'Have a look at these [visual]. Put up your hand [kinaesthetic] if you think we're selling baked beans. Now raise your hand to tell me (auditory) if you think we are selling bananas. Thank you. The answer is that we are selling

bananas. We can carry four hundred bananas on a train but they are perishable and have a sell-by date. So do our seats.'

Having started with this creative opening, Shulla was able to return to beans and bananas throughout the presentation. She had also been doing some research on the way transport is 'sold' across the world and had planned to show numerous PowerPoint slides to illustrate it.

Chris helped her to jettison that idea and bring the presentation to life. She used the stage area that she had to represent the countries in the world that she had studied. She moved across her stage to map out each country, so that her audience knew that when she went to front and stage left she was in China, front and stage right was the USA. As she visited each country she changed her accent or her posture to emphasise the difference. The audience felt as though they were experiencing each country with her.

Shula enjoyed the creativity that Chris helped her find and was aware that the audience appreciated it too. She knew she had made an impact when beans and bananas were referred to for the duration of the meeting.

Chris was encouraging Shula to use what's known as 'spatial marking' in this second part of her presentation. Spacial marking is a form of anchoring on the platform and can be used to great effect. Imagine you knew that your presentation would have some theory that required note taking, some practical small group work and some fun stories. You can decide where on your platform to put each of these elements so that your audience would know that, when you go to stage right, you will expect them to move into break out groups, when you move into centre stage they will know it is time to listen and, if they want to, to have their notebooks ready, and when you are in stage left that is where the jokes and funny stories come from. Centre stage is the most powerful position on the stage, so this is where you make your positive impression on your audience. Experiment with marking your stage, whatever size it is, as part of your preparation and notice what happens if you stick to the same place for different aspects. It is fun and as you watch your audience react you will know they have unconsciously got the message. It will also indicate that you are in rapport with your audience which of course makes the whole process simpler for you.

Mental rehearsal

Mental rehearsal is practice in the imagination which prepares and primes the body for an actual situation. Giving the brain strong positive images of success programmes it to think in those terms and makes success more likely. It is a technique that involves imagined, mental practice of performing a task as opposed to actual practice. When you engage in mental rehearsal, you imagine performing without having to go anywhere or do anything. You visualise what is seen, heard, felt, smelt and tasted as you practise in your mind.

As the saying goes: 'Practice makes perfect.' Yes, practice can cause improvement, but 'perfect practice' can lead to better results than practice full of failures. Because mental practice is perfect practice, it is also a confidence booster. The reason visual imagery works lies in the fact that when you imagine yourself performing to perfection and doing precisely what you want, you are in turn physiologically creating neural patterns in your brain, just as if you had physical performed the action. These patterns are similar to small tracks engraved in the brain cells which can ultimately enable an athlete to perform physical feats by simply mentally practicing the move. Hence, mental imagery is intended to train our minds and create the neural patterns in our brain to teach our muscles to do exactly what we want them to do. Experiencing success increases confidence, even if that experience is imagined.

This is a technique that is widely used in NLP to help you run through what you want in your mind before experiencing the actual event. You know how powerful your unconscious mind is and this is a way of harnessing that power and using it to work for you. High achievers in business, theatre, music and sport have a vivid idea in their minds of what they want to achieve: shaking hands when the big deal is agreed or standing on the podium singing their country's national anthem. And if you were to ask them about the idea, they will usually be able to describe it vividly and in detail. They already know what it will be like. The mind and body are so closely linked that they are a formidable force when they are working together to help you in any situation, not just presentations and meetings. Much of the research into the efficacy of mental rehearsal has been carried out in the sporting arena.

One experiment took a group of basketball players and divided them into three groups. The first group were supervised to physically practice regularly, the second group were not to practice at all and the third group only visualised daily successful practice. After three weeks the groups were re-tested for the effects of their varying degrees of activity. Group 1 had improved by 2 per cent; group 2, not surprisingly, had deteriorated by 2 per cent, and group three had improved by 3.5 per cent. Their minds couldn't tell the difference between what they were vividly imagining and reality. Try it out for yourself before you next present or are facing an uncomfortable meeting, and find out how well it works.

Mentally rehearse your presentation

1. Have a specific goal in your mind. What do you want to happen at the presentation or meeting? How do you want to feel and how do you want the audience to feel? How do you want them to be at the end of your time? Imagine a huge and positive response with everyone standing and clapping as you finish. If it is appropriate, imagine them laughing enthusiastically at your jokes. Imagine them learning, growing and developing as they take in the messages you want to convey. You will start to feel the way you would feel if you got those responses. And that feels good!

2. Find a time and place where you won't be interrupted.

3. Sit down or lie comfortably and let yourself relax.

4. Relax, concentrate and focus. Take deep breaths and exhale slowly. Free your mind from distractions as you focus on the relaxation process.

5. Once relaxed, focus on the specific challenging task.

6. Mentally tell yourself that you are confident and that you have the ability to perform this task successfully. Repeatedly tell yourself, with confidence, that you will be successful. Use all your senses so that you can see, hear, smell, taste, touch and feel the emotions that ensure success.

7. Imagine what you will see, hear and feel, just before you begin the presentation. Visualise yourself as an active participant, not as a passive observer. For example, to mentally rehearse the start of your presentation, imagine that you are standing in front of your audience, rather than watching yourself as you stand.

8. Remaining relaxed and focused, mentally rehearse successful performance of this task. Imagine going through the process and seeing, hearing and feeling your successful results.

9. Enjoy yourself in your rehearsal. It's important that you do.

10. Finally, open your eyes and smile. You have successfully performed in your mind, which is great preparation for actual performance. You should now be confident that you will perform successfully in the real situation. Remember to praise yourself for being successful. Self-reinforcement is another a key to self-motivation.

11. Practice regularly, five minutes a day, once a day for a week before the presentation and notice the difference in your confidence and clarity.

Conclusion

- **Research for rapport** – Find out what kind of state your audience is likely to be in. If possible talk to some of the main protagonists before the meeting, work out how they tick and what they want. Is the organisation in flux, stable or going through expansion? Fit your presentation to match.

- **Assume some positive beliefs** – 'I am in charge and this is my opportunity to put across my ideas.' 'They have asked me to speak because they believe I have the knowledge. They appreciate my expertise.' 'They are on my side and want me to succeed.' 'This is my team and we can succeed together.'

- Fire your **anchors** from start to finish, stay resourceful.

- **State management** – Know what state you want yourself to be in and how to you will achieve it. Plan to change your and their states as you present.
- **Breathe** deeply from your diaphragm and regularly, rather than quickly and from your chest. You want as much oxygen going to your brain as possible. If you start to feel shaky put your tongue on the base of your mouth and it will help to calm you.
- **Loosen** up your jaw, your mouth, your tongue, your neck and your shoulders. All these muscles need warming up, just like a runner's legs.
- **Loosen** and **vary your vocals** – you need variety of pitch and tone for the auditories in your audience. Humming and tongue twisters can help here.
- Make sure you are **hydrated** and have water if you need it (though not too much!).
- **Silent beginning** – Don't rush into your brilliant opening as soon as you reach centre stage (and definitely not beforehand). Stand and ground yourself for about 20 seconds. Claim your place on the whatever platform and give your audience time to settle too.
- **Be yourself** – You will be much more effective and have a better audience reaction if you are authentic. It's easier for you too.
- **Take care of yourself** – Make sure you are well rested and well prepared – this will help you and give you the confidence you need to answer questions. It also gives you the best chance to shine and be your best.
- At the start, **mention the advantages** they will gain: 'In order for our team to work better together and for this project to run move smoothly ...'
- **Get feedback** – Make a conscious effort to arrange for feedback from one or two people you can trust to be honest and constructive. Listen and accept what has

worked well and consider what you will do with any development points made.

- **Model and learn** – Consider who has inspired you with their speeches or team talks in the past. Who represents your model of best practice? If you can still watch and listen to them, do so and interview them to find out how they do what they do. What aspects of their presenting can you incorporate into your own style?

- **Enjoy!** – This can be one of the most rewarding things you can do in your job. It is wonderful when you know that your team is listening to you and interacting with you. It's a privilege.

INSTANT TIP

Remember that your presentation is simply a **conversation** between you and a few other people.

09

What would make appraisals work better?

For the purposes of this book I am taking appraisals to represent a meeting that is longer and more structured than the spontaneous coaching intervention I outlined in Chapter 7. The skills, processes and techniques from both chapters are interchangeable and are all aimed to help you broaden your communications and make them even more successful. This is not a chapter about the structure and stages of an appraisal meeting, more a selection of tools to increase your confidence and flexibility in the meeting.

Appraisals are an opportunity to elicit expectations, set goals and handle any obstructions that could prevent your staff from achieving their goals. Here are a few ideas to help you think about how you might achieve what you want from the meeting.

- To elicit their perception of their role – 'Before we start the appraisal I'm just wondering what your thoughts are on how you see your role and where you add value to the company?'

● To elicit ways to further utilise skills and resources – 'You are a crucial member of this department and at the same time I don't know if there are any ideas you have that if they were implemented would add even more value to the team'

● To identify changes to roles or responsibilities to utilise skills – 'On a scale of 1 to 10, with 10 being an exact fit for what you are looking for in a role and 1 being no fit whatsoever, where do you feel your current role fits with your idea of a perfect role that would utilise your skills while being the kind of role that would give you a great deal of job satisfaction' (Generally, the answer will be between 6 and 8.) This allows you to ask for the key distinctions that will enable positive changes to be made to the role, responsibilities or environment by asking: 'What would need to be different in your role for the fit to be 10 out of 10?' This enables the employee to articulate changes or ideas without it seeming that they are being criticised or threatened.

● On pre-handling objections to targets – 'If at the end of the next 6 months you wouldn't have been able to meet these targets what do you think the most likely reasons for that would be?' You can then identify whether or not those objections are within the control of the employee or outside factors. If the key hurdles to the targets can be handled during the 6 months then the targets are perceived to be more achievable within the mind of the team member.

Frames

Frames are how you contextualise what is going on around you. Your map of the world is made up of many frames which will unconsciously lead you to certain actions and reactions. We each frame the world in our own unique way, so that two people who witness the same events may interpret them differently. The facts of an exchange might be indisputable, the frames attributed to the exchange can be as different as the number of people who are involved in it or observe it.

> For example, Sam is a manager who, by his own admission, is not a 'people person'. He is great at his job and wholeheartedly supports his team knowing that they are highly skilled and capable people. A new member joining his team framed him as insensitive because he rarely looked in to see how she was doing. She had to approach him for help. A colleague who joined the company at the same as Sam time framed him as the best boss because he let them get on with their work and was always there if needed. The management framed him as top team material because of the hours he put into the business and the results he achieved. Sam's wife and children framed him as Mr Invisible because he often missed out on their family activities due to work commitments.

When an actor is described as being 'typecast', it means that they always seem to play the same sort of character. Sometimes they feel the need to step out of type outrageously to extend themselves and their repertoire. Their audiences find it difficult to accept them in the new frame. They believe the actor has the 'old' attributes and can't change. Daniel Radcliffe caused ructions when he exchanged the role of Harry Potter (sweet child wizard extraordinaire), for the sadistic horse torturer in 'Equus'. Ronald Reagan never quite lost his 'charming actor' persona when he went into politics, and was accused of being 'directed' and 'learning his lines' rather than being true to himself throughout his presidency. They were both potentially stuck in frames that could make them one dimensional.

The same thing may be happening in your business, where one team member is regularly overlooked to make presentations because they are so quiet and unassuming. No-one knows that they regularly act as spokesperson for the charity they support. They are just not in the frame.

The way you frame something determines to a large degree the meaning you attach to it. Based on their different priorities and frames of reference, each person interprets what they see and hear in a manner that is unique to them. The point is for you as a manager to recognise this in yourself and accept that yours is just one of a number of possible interpretations. If you are unwilling or unable to do so, you are severely limiting yourself and your team. Later on in this chapter you can consider what happens when you change the frame, then you and your team can challenge behaviours that no longer support you.

In NLP there are five information frames that are most commonly used and which provide: a focus for your activities; a way to check that you are behaving congruently; a context in which you can assess your progress; opportunities to explore other possibilities; and a way to ensure a common understanding. You can use them to clarify or focus your own thinking, or that of your appraisees, your team or your customers. These frames will be an asset to your appraisal interviews because they will help you and your appraisee to check that they are progressing in the most proficient way.

Outcome frame

This is a frame that was mentioned in Chapter 1 and is a cornerstone of NLP thinking. You and your team need to know what you want you want and what you are each working towards. For an outcome to be well formed, it has to be framed positively and in a way that enables you to keep evaluating it. If you and your team find yourselves off course, you can agree to do something different and make necessary changes. If you have nothing to aim at, that is what you are likely to achieve.

Make sure that you and your team members have clear outcomes for the appraisal meeting, then be sure to consult and discuss them well before you meet. This will save time at the beginning and ensure that you both get at least some of what you want from the meeting. If you decide on your outcome alone and present it for the first time at the appraisal, your team member may feel undermined and become unco-operative. By working out shared and agreed outcomes for the meeting you will have demonstrated your rapport skills and indicated to your appraisee that you already welcome and value their contribution. You will also have a solid foundation for future progress and decision-making between you both. You can use the outcome frame to help you and your team member set objectives by checking that they are set in the positive, are specific, have evidence against which to be measured, fits in with other outcomes, are under their control and that you have defined some action steps to make them happen.

The outcome frame has another application when it is contrasted with a problem frame. As its name suggests, a problem frame will focus you and your appraisee on what is wrong, needs fixing, or is not working, rather than on what is desired or how to create solutions. Chapter 7 described how talking in terms of problems can open negative files in your mind which affects your internal dialogue and your approach. It also tends to keep you in the past. This can, of course, be useful when you want to understand the cause of a non-conformance, as long as you have the flexibility to move into an outcome frame to move forward into solutions.

Notice how you feel and what ideas form in your mind when you consider an issue from inside a problem or an outcome frame. In the following example I have included a couple of 'blaming' questions because the problem frame often moves responsibility outside a person and it's good to know whether this is what you or your appraisees are doing.

Think about an issue that is of mild concern for you and that it would be useful for you to change. Answer the questions below for the same situation and notice how they affect you differently.

PROBLEM FRAME	OUTCOME FRAME
What is the problem?	What do I want?
How long have I had it?	How will I know when I've got it?
Who do I normally blame?	What will improve when I've got it?
Whose fault is it really?	What stops me from having my desired outcome already?
How does this problem limit me?	What resources do I already have that can help achieve this outcome?
What is the worst experience of this problem?	What is something similar in which I have succeeded?
Why haven't I solved it yet?	What is the next step or steps?

You will also find the results differ dramatically when you take the focus of the frame away from problems and towards any corrections that have already been made or could be made in future to improve or remove them.

In *The Solutions Focus: Making Coaching and Change SIMPLE* (2007), Paul Z. Jackson and Mark McKergow describe how an Italian chemical plant used a solutions frame to persuade their staff to wear the mandatory safety glasses

The managers (and the law) wanted people to wear safety glasses. The workers were nevertheless reluctant. The solution emerged when someone asked themselves, 'When does this future perfect even partially occur? When do our people wear glasses anyway, even when they don't strictly need to?' We're talking Italian men here. When do Italian men wear glasses when they don't need to? When they are cool, fashionable sunglasses!

So they commissioned a set of safety glasses with mirror shades, and offered them to operators on the factory floor. And a miracle did happen: the workers instantly began wearing them most of the time, even outside the chemically hazardous areas. From just a small change in the design came this significant change in behaviour.

The firm could have chosen a problem focus instead: it could have studied the reasons for people not wearing the old safety glasses, their motivations for risking themselves and their health or the underlying causes of accidents around the world. Would this solution have emerged from such an inquiry? We guess not.

Ecology frame

This frame ensures that all the consequences of an outcome are considered as in the notion of 'fit' mentioned in the outcomes section of Chapter 1. If you have a gut reaction that something doesn't seem right, but you have no hard evidence, trust it and use the ecology frame to check things through. Using this frame also enables you and your appraisee to consider the impact of their actions on the wider systems outside themselves. You might ask them such questions as; 'Who else is likely to be affected by this decision?', 'What other consequences might there be if we make this decision?'

Evidence frame

This concentrates on clear and specific details and is a way of ensuring that whatever you are doing is grounded in reality. It is also part of the outcome model and tests for sensory evidence. What evidence is there to determine how far you are from your outcomes? How will you know when you have achieved your outcome. What will you see, hear and feel? You will find this frame of reference helps you to test your assumptions and actions.

As-if frame

This is a frame that stimulates creativity and allows you and your appraisee to enhance your perception of what is possible. It is based on acting 'as if' a desired state or outcome has been achieved, or 'as if' someone else is giving you information, or behaving 'as if' you were someone else and modelling them from second position. I often have groups project themselves ten years into the future. They behave as if their business is being heralded as the best there is and everyone wants to know what did they over the past ten years to become so successful. This immediately frees them from the constraints and challenges of now and allows them to use their imagination and unconscious minds. It is a resourceful activity that has the added benefit of giving them an insight into the options available.

It can be used in a number of ways that enable you to suspend your disbelief and try on different scenarios until you find one that fits. Because this is supposedly not real only 'as if', people will often feel freer and more able to let their thoughts run without censure. 'What would happen if we had the finances in place?' You can use this frame to help your appraisee weigh up the pros and cons of a decision they have to make. They can consider what it would be like if the worst happened and what would they do if the best thing happened. Both these deliberations will give them a clearer idea of which way they want to go. The exercise at the end of this chapter widens the possibilities of reframing and using the 'as if' frame to creatively solve a problem.

Backtrack frame

This frame will prove a useful checking device as you go through the appraisal. It builds on the rapport you will have established by demonstrating to your appraisee that you are actively listening to them and are in their world. In a backtrack frame you repeat back to your appraisee the information you have received so far, and you use the appraisee's key words, pace, phrasing and tonality to do so. Saying them back to your appraisee will give both of you an insight into their meaning. You will have a better appreciation of what is important and what matters to them. This is different from a summary or paraphrase because they both include an element of interpretation on your part. It is also a good way to check that you both understand and agree the actions that will follow. The backtrack frame is also useful in other meetings when you want to clarify the present position and start to move forward.

Reframing

'You can't stop the waves, but you can learn to surf.' Jack Kornfield

My friend Stephanie is a brilliant reframer. She loves going to antique markets and, as far as I am concerned, she buys a lot of old junk. She comes back with many pictures that are fairly ordinary and tells me she has bought them for the frames. Once she swaps the pictures around and puts them in different frames, the results are amazing. Her house is decorated with fabulous pictures that have been transformed by their frame.

The frames of reference that you choose as a result of your beliefs about yourself and others, your perceived role in life or your perceived limitations in skills/abilities can limit what you consider possible or can open up all sorts of possibilities. Of course, reframing is not unique to NLP, it is something we do a lot of the time. I am often reminded of this when I work with people facing redundancy. Their initial reactions can be fear and anxiety. In retrospect, many often feel it is the best thing that ever happened and they wished they had left earlier. It is the people who have been left behind who may have more issues to deal with.

Changing the frame of an experience can have a major influence on how you perceive, interpret and react to that experience. I was working with Anya, who wanted to get rid of her obsessive behaviour as she was frightened it would stall her progress in her first job. 'How do you know it's obsessive?' 'Because when I was young I would get heavily involved in anything that interested me. I would read books about and collect articles on the subject and talk about it non stop. Dad was sick of all the bits and pieces around it.' I reflected that I might describe the behaviour as *enthusiastic* and that I would be delighted if she applied such keenness to her work. Anya's physiology changed and she visibly relaxed. She had reframed her behaviour from 'obsessive' to 'enthusiastic', which gave her a completely different sense of herself. This illustrates how a change in frame can have a

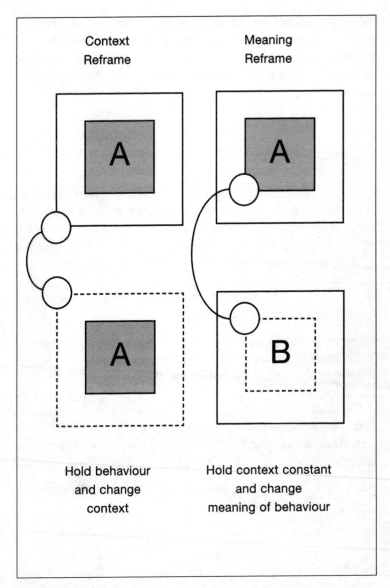

Figure 9.1: Reframing

significant impact on the choices you make. In the appraisal meeting you can use reframing when your appraisee seems stuck in their thinking about an issue. If you can help them to put the issue into a different frame, they might be able to change their perception.

Context reframing

Context reframing enables you to recognise that there is a positive place for almost any behaviour – doing the right thing in the right place at the right time. Embarrassment is sometimes simply the result of getting the time or place wrong. Next time you find yourself or someone else limiting themselves with phrases like 'I'm too sensitive, too careless, too slow', or 'I wish I could stop doing ...'. Use reframe questions to find a context in which the behaviour is appropriate and positive.

Q. 'When would it be beneficial to be sensitive?'
A. 'When I notice someone in the office who is nervous or unsure.'

Q. 'Where would being slow be an advantage?'
A. 'In a meeting that is making decisions about budgets.'

An excuse is a reframe that attributes a different meaning or context to your behaviours.

Content reframing

Content reframing is where you can change the meaning of a seemingly limiting behaviour. Comedians do this often with 'good news, bad news' jokes. Less humorously, perhaps, the good news is that sales have increased by 50 per cent in the last quarter. The bad news is that staff are complaining about the increased hours and no extra personnel to meet demands.

You might want to use content framing next time you hear statements like, 'My mind goes blank when I stand up to make a presentation', or 'I get upset when I make mistakes'. Your aim is to find another, more useful meaning.

Q. 'What else could going blank mean?'
A. 'It could mean I'm clearing my mind to concentrate on what I want to say.'

Q. 'What is the value of getting upset?'
A. 'It shows how much pride I take in doing a job well.'

Politicians are masters at reframing. It seems no matter what happens, they can put a positive spin on it for themselves and a negative spin for their opponents. I often think about the fact that the Chinese have two words that respond to our word for chaos. They consider it an opportunity or a threat. Whichever way you reframe, it will lead to very different behavioural and emotional consequences.

Metaphor

'Shall I compare thee to a summer's day? Thou art more lovely and more temperate.' William Shakespeare

There is no doubt that William Shakespeare knew a lot about metaphors and how to use them to engage people's emotions. They create a state of inventiveness, openness and acceptance. They are also a another type of reframe because they offer you the opportunity to move from a seemingly fixed position to one full of options and new insights.

'We need to compare things to understand. Metaphors make us think about one thing in terms of another; they bring life to the literal and make abstract concepts more tangible. Our understanding becomes richer and more complete through metaphor.' Sue Lickorish

I love to use metaphors in all aspects of the work I do. In presentations they are a way of putting people into the state you want them to access. Rather that telling them to relax, I might slow my speech and ask them to imagine they are on sandy beach listening to the water gently lapping near their feet, watching the sun go down and feeling at peace with the world around them. What state do you want your appraisee to be in at the meeting? Start with a metaphor to agree and elicit that state and you will both be more resourceful. Ask them 'what would this meeting be like if were to be successful for us both?'. If you think they might be nervous or unsure, you could tell them a story about your first appraisal and how you were apprehensive to begin and how your manager put you at ease from the very start etc. Or tell them how a first appraisal reminds you of someone's first day at work, which started full of confusion and by the end of it they wondered what they had been worrying about.

My colleague Tracy Plaice, author of *Face the Music and Win – How to Follow Your Passion and Conquer Your Fear*, likes to reconnect people to their dreams and passion in the workplace as well as outside. She tells a story of her near death accident that left her with a badly broken right hand. As a child, Tracy was passionate about playing a piano, but was unable to share her talent with others for fear of making a mistake and not being 'good enough'. Though she studied up to the top grade, when she left home, 18 years had passed without her playing a piano, but always promising herself that she would get back to it 'one day'. When she seemed to have left it too late, she was angry that procrastination and fear had got in the way of something she loved. Determined that fear would no longer dictate her actions, she vowed to get back to playing a piano and learn how to conquer her fear of performance. Within a year of that decision she played solos in seven concerts including an international performance. Her story is one of courage and determination and breaking through psychological barriers. When Tracy is working with other people, her main question to them is 'what is the piano in your life?'

Using metaphors in the appraisal meeting will assist your appraisee to address some tricky issues from a position that is one step removed from the actual situation which will make it seem less risky. When they tell you that they feel as though they are wading through treacle, it is much more descriptive and informative than just telling you they feel stuck. There a number of ways of responding. You can ask them to describe their journey in the treacle so far. How thick is it? How deep is it? What does it taste like? To stay in rapport you can agree that it must seem as though any progress will be slow and a great effort, a really sticky state of affairs. If your appraisee is not able to describe their relationship to a person or situation, ask them for a metaphor. How are they like a car, an animal, a piece of fruit or a Hollywood film? What are the attributes relating to the situation and how close are they to how you feel about it?

When I worked as a student counsellor for 16 to 19-year-olds, they were not always able to articulate their feelings and what was making them feel bad. They were very adept at comparing their situation to that of their favourite television 'soap' and between us we could agree how that character might proceed in order to change the way they were living their lives.

The business world is full of metaphors – sometimes they are used as euphemisms for the less popular facts. I am amused by people who take 'gardening leave', who are in fact usually being paid a large sum of money to work out a notice period before going to a rival company. Their present employers do not want them stealing or storing ideas for their new ones and they do not want them going straight over to them either. Start to notice whether there are any particular metaphors that relate to your business and your team. What are their implications and do you want to change them? Are you working in an *urban jungle*, do you run a *tight ship* or are you expected to *keep your cards close to your chest*?

A colleague, Francesca Guilia Mereu, was working with a new manager, Cristini, who was nervous about giving appraisals to his team. He was an emotionally intelligent young man working for an international bank. He did not like to give negative feedback when his staff were under-performing. His staff felt cheated and that they were not developing in the required competences. They thought he was not a real leader and resented the fact that he never told them the facts in a straightforward way. They were becoming disrespectful and he found it increasingly hard to set objectives with them. Francesca decided to try some mental rehearsal. She asked Cristini to imagine watching himself on a movie screen, giving appraisals in terms of behaviour and goals and not about personality. To find the words in a kind way whilst still telling what needed to be said. To hear himself describing what someone was or was not doing and to feel comfortable sitting with them at the meeting. She encouraged him to imagine himself behaving as though he was already supremely skilled in giving feedback and as though his staff appreciated the chance to have his opinion and learn new ways of working. As he became more comfortable and relaxed, Francesca suggested that he move into the Cristini on the screen and really start to experience the appraisals he wanted. Cristini practised with the visualisation daily and was much more comfortable with his new way of managing poor performance. It was no longer scary and so no longer a big deal for him.

This is an excellent way for you to practice managing appraisal meetings before you have to conduct them for real. You can also ask a senior manager and your own appraiser for some advice on what works best for them. Compare your appraisals to a garden, a mode of transport or anything that particularly interests you and that will change its impact on you.

Adam Cox, associate director of Radio Relations, uses metaphors to elicit motivational incentives in his appraisals:

'I have a member of staff who in her appraisal when we were talking about motivation, requested a guinea pig for the office. Targets were set on the condition that, if she met her targets, she would get a guinea pig that would belong within the business but she could still see it at work. Since she was not motivated by financial incentives, it did not make sense to have anything other than the thing she was motivated towards. Now whenever I want to elicit the key thing which is not money

that my staff would want more than anything else, I ask them to tell me what is their "guinea pig". The story of Luisa explains the outcome I am looking for (a non-financial incentive), while still being a way to break their pattern and elicit something that, although not likely to cost the company too much money, will still prove to be motivating possibly even compelling to the member of staff.'

Storytelling

Storytelling is an integral part of NLP and falls into the metaphor category. Stories describe something that happens in a different time or place from whatever is your present. They bypass the conscious mind and move people emotionally to greater understanding and action. The details of a report may be forgotten, but the stories are retained and repeated. This book is deliberately full of stories and metaphors to illustrate the different concepts. They bring the theory to life and often add an extra understanding because you can create your meaning from someone else's experience.

Stories were central to an annual housing trust team meeting I helped facilitate. There had been a significant change in the top team membership and there was unrest. The day started with a short film with a mix of tenants telling their special stories and describing what living in one of the housing trust's home meant to them. The effect was immense. The staff laughed and cried and then remembered why they were working with the organisation. They were galvanised into action and had a brilliant and affirming day which broke down some of the previous barriers to progress.

Appraisals are a great place to find out what the stories are in your team and how they affect each team member. Asking your appraisee for examples of good customer service, best and worst managers or their ideal appraisal meeting is encouraging them to give you a story of their experiences. Outside the appraisal meeting you will encounter stories on your email, around the water cooler and in the pub after the day has finished. Listen to them and find out how what their underlying messages are about your business and people's perceptions of it.

I use the stories of my experiences from appearing in pantomime to illustrate a number of NLP concepts. I talk about the way different ways the 'teams' interact, the props team need clear procedures to make sure every scene is set correctly, the make-up team want a vague idea and then to be left to their own devices. I describe how the actors decide what states they want to elicit from the audience and how to find it in themselves. I ask my audience to consider who are the heroes in their organisation and who are the villains. I also compare the different styles of directors I have experienced and how their feedback and appraisal of my performance had helped or hindered me.

Conclusion

Think about an appraisal issue that you have struggled with in the past or that you anticipate may affect you in the future. I would like to offer you a reframing exercise that will help you to change perspectives and enable you to create many options and insights about the issue. When you have an issue or situation to work with, consider it from the following perspectives:

1. How might the issue be perceived by the following and what might they say to you:

● A friend who is accepting and respectful.
● A mentor.
● A curious, adventuresome five-year-old child.
● An alien, perhaps from Mars ... or Venus.

- A person who would think the opposite to you about the situation.
  If you were 10 or 20 years younger, how would you respond differently now?
  If you were 10 or 20 years older, how would you respond differently now?
  If the situation were humorous, what would you be laughing about?
  What is the bigger picture that this is only a part of?

2. Now ... consider:

- What are you going to be doing since you have changed?
- How do you perceive the situation differently now?
- What new and different possibilities are there now as a result of taking multiple perceptions?

INSTANT TIP

Help your appraisees reframe their challenges to make them more manageable.

10

How can I reduce my own and my staff's stress and increase productivity?

Stress is often given a bad press. Whilst I would agree that, in the main, it has negative connotations, I would also like to recognise when it is positive. Stress can be facilitating or debilitating and whichever it is depends on many variables. If I didn't have a target date – which in some ways leads me to feel stressed – I would probably not have finished (or maybe even started) writing this book. If I didn't have butterflies in my stomach before going on stage or before making a business pitch, I would be missing the adrenalin needed to perform at my peak. Not sleeping at night and losing my car keys are signs to me of debilitating stress that I need to get to the root of and make some changes. The key is deciding which stressors you want to reduce and which you want to embrace, enjoy and work with. The next step is to determine how to put some balance checks in place to accommodate rest and renewal time. Even the facilitating form of stress can become damaging and lead to illness, if you stay on a perpetual adrenalin fuelled high.

'Pay attention to and consciously relax the micro tensions in your body. They are like the light bulbs left on in your house. One bulb might not make much impact, but if you leave the lights on in every room, you will waste a lot of energy.' Francesca Giulia Mereu

Our cave-dwelling ancestors had the right idea, through necessity rather than the benefits of research, when they put most of their adrenalin and energies into finding, killing and dragging their food back to the cave. Everyone would eat their fill and then go into a state of recovery and relaxation before setting off on another food hunt. They appreciated the need for renewal and recharge time to ensure they were in prime condition for their next encounter. Some wild animals are the same – they catch their food, eat it and rest until they become hungry again. I often think how uncomplicated it would be living as a lion, lazing around in the warmth of the Serengeti with complete confidence that my family and I would find food when we needed it and could enjoy snoozing in the sun for most of the rest of the time. I realise this is both anthropomorphic and pure fantasy. From an NLP perspective, though, it gives me some clear indications of where to locate my outcomes and visualisations. As it is, we are situated in the 24/7 society, with increasingly intrusive communication mechanisms, to which we can be 'on call' all day, every day if we don't draw clear boundaries. No wonder people complain of being stressed and their performance levels drop. Being promoted to team leader means that you will have taken on greater responsibilities and senior staff will expect more from you. It is even more important now that you look after yourself so that you can look after your team.

I was working with a group of senior R&D managers from a multinational company. They were expected to check emails and make phone calls until late at night to catch their American business counterparts, and then, from early in the morning, to be there for the Japanese. Another client had been given a Blackberry device by her boss and she was expected to answer emails and text messages into her evening and beyond. It seems that businesses can no longer wait for anything. They need an answer NOW. How did we ever manage before the internet and mobile phones? How can companies expect their employees to remain at optimum productivity if they do not have time for rest and relaxation to recharge their batteries before the next day's work?

The idea of nominalisations was introduced as a meta model deletion in Chapter 2. It occurs when you take a verb which is active and turn it into a noun which makes it fixed and passive. This can leaves the word open to interpretation and assumption. Once you turn the noun back into a verb, it becomes effective again and there is scope for change. Stress is a normalisation that is prevalent in the workplace today. To me, and in its negative frame, the noun 'stress' suggests a state of being uptight and overwhelmed. To you it may mean something quite different. So, it is a great idea to ask precise, meta model questions to understand how it affects you and your team:

- What's stressing you?
- Who's stressing you?
- How are you stressing yourself?
- What do you get out of being stressed and how could you achieve the same result in another way?
- How could you de-stress yourself? What would you look like, sound like and feel like?
- Are you stressing anyone in your team?

These questions will stimulate some deep thought and the answers will give you an excellent starting point for addressing the issues raised. If you know that you don't want to be stressed, what do you want instead? What would you be doing, looking like, sounding and feeling like if you were not stressed?

Executive and Personal Performance coach, Maria Deacon-Viney, tells of Eric, a manager she was coaching. He would go through phases of being very stressed when his inner dialogue was very damning of himself and his team. In one session he was feeling desperate because he had 'missed his targets on absolutely everything'. Knowing this to be highly unlikely, Maria challenged this generalisation and asked Eric which targets, exactly, had he not met. In a very short time they had established that he had hit 75 per cent of his targets and was focusing on a particularly challenging 25 per cent. Maria also challenged him to reflect on the kind of message his exaggeration was giving his team. Suggesting that they were missing all their targets would be demoralising and could lead to lack of motivation. She supported Eric in his decision to praise the fact that they had reached a fabulous 75 per cent and ask them to put the same energy and endeavour into the more demanding 25 per cent. She was encouraging Eric and his team to change their focus from what was not working to what was. That would immediately put them into a more resourceful state, from which they could tackle what remained to be done. We know that NLP places great store on the mind / body connection, and whilst Eric's team's minds were in a negative place, their bodies would seem lethargic and immobile.

Focus on what you want. Tell yourself and others what you want, not what you don't want. If someone asks 'How are you?', reply with 'good' or even better 'excellent', while using a tone of voice that shows you mean it. Notice how much better this feels than saying 'Not bad'.

'Before I was paralysed there were 10,000 things I could do. Now there are 9,000. I can either dwell on the 1,000 I've lost or focus on the 9,000 I have left.' W. Mitchell, keynote speaker

You too can start to notice what you and your team members focus on and what effect this has. What makes some of your team members more laid back and relaxed than their colleagues? The answer is *perception*. Your map of the world defines the meaning you give to the events in your office or outside. This is what shapes your thoughts and feelings, either stressfully or in a more accepting way. Other people or situations that occur do not stress or relax you, it is how you react to them that has the effect. If I rephrase what Eleanor Roosevelt said: 'no-one can make you feel stressed without your consent.' In Chapter 7 I suggested that you might want to collect your nuggets of gold throughout the day. Too many of us are practiced at the negative focus – we do that without thinking. Collecting the positives is another way to ensure you make a conscious decision to focus on what works and is going well for you. When you list or record what you are happy with inside and outside work, it will stay with you.

Submodalities

Chapter 4 outlined representational systems and how they are an expression of the way we think and process information. Within each of these systems we make finer distinctions which give us more data about the quality of our experiences. In NLP these distinctions are called submodalities and they describe how we refine our sensory experiences. They are the foundation stones of the senses, characterising how each picture, sound, feeling, taste and smell is composed.

Submodalities are how we code experiences and distinguish different sensory systems.

Submodalities make the difference between an experience you remember as positive and one which you would rather forget or which makes you cringe when you recall it. Once you recognise your preferred method of coding, you can choose whether or not to change the code. This is particularly useful when you want to replace a stressful state with a more motivated one or to lessen the impact of a painful past event. Some people tend to store their memories in a way that leads to negative, low-energy reactions or anticipates future events with worry and anxiety. By changing their submodalities, they can shift their whole experience. If you feel down or negative, you tap into your unhappy memory 'bins', which will lead to more unhappy feelings and a spiral being created as more bin lids are opened. If you feel happy, you tap into the happy memory bins. The mind wants to give you congruence by supporting you with evidence that supports your feelings.

What is different about those days you just can't seem to get out of bed and those when you are up bright and early, raring to go? Some people see the day ahead as dark, cold and all they can hear is a morbid drone. On their good days everything is brighter, they feel full of energy and enjoy listening to the birds singing sweetly. Once you recognise the words that describe your 'good' days, you can choose how to use them. You can choose to access them more often to reduce your stress and increase your feeling of well-being.

- Think about a task that you don't like. As you do so, notice whether you recall pictures of the task, the words or sounds associated with it or the accompanying feelings.
- Write down or record a description of what came into your mind and be as detailed as you can. Stop thinking about that experience, move around, change state and think of something else.
- This time, think about a task you really enjoy and take on with vigour. As you do so, notice whether you recall pictures of the task, the words or sounds associated with it or the accompanying feelings.
- Write down or record a description of what came into your mind and be as detailed as you can. Stop

> thinking about that experience, move around,
> change state and come back to now.
> ● Compare the lists and notice what kind of words you
> have used to describe your motivated and
> unmotivated states. Which submodalities are the
> difference which makes the difference?

What you have now is an indication of the way your thinking about a situation can make it pleasurable or not. If you accept that a memory is simply that – an event that happened and cannot be changed – why spend time wallowing in the bad moments and letting them influence the way you run your life? By changing your submodalities, you can change the impact and meaning of your thoughts. You can also change your approach to any outstanding tasks.

Your submodality distinctions may have included:

Visual
- Colour – black and white or shaded tones.
- Brightness – dullness or shininess.
- Clarity – dim and hazy or sharp and in focus.
- Size – larger than life, lifesize or smaller.
- Framed or panoramic.
- Location – in front, to one side or behind you.
- Clarity – blurred or in focus.
- Associated – seen through your own eyes, as if you are inside the experience.
- Dissociated – looking, from the outside, at yourself in the picture.

Auditory
- Volume – loud or quiet.
- Words or sounds.

- Stereo, mono or surround sound.
- Distance – close or from afar.
- Tone – soft or harsh and whose voice(s)?
- Speed – faster or slower than usual.

Kinaesthetic
- Pressure – hard, soft or sense of being pushed.
- Texture – rough or smooth.
- Weight – light or heavy.
- Location – where in your body do you experience sensations?
- Shape – angular or curved.
- Intensity – strong or weak.

- Go back to the task that was not one of your favourites.
- As you think about it, this time consciously make it bigger and closer to you. Imagine yourself doing it rather than watching on from the outside. Use a positive pitch to tell yourself how good it will be when you have done it. Imagine feeling satisfied with a great sense of achievement.
- Play around with *your* submodalities and notice the way they change the impact on you.

You can make changes in any situations. If you don't like the result, change them back or try something different.

There are some general trends in the submodalities connected with feeling stressed. The pictures are probably monochrome, blurred and one dimensional. You will be watching yourself as an observer. The sounds are likely to be muted, slow and dull. Your feelings will be of not belonging, weakness and stillness. In the case of feeling confident and motivated, pictures tend to be associated, big and bright. Sounds are clear and normal pace. Feelings will be solid and warm. The way we talk about our inner thoughts also reflects our mood. For example: 'I always look on the bright side' rather than 'the future looks black'.

I was working with a junior executive who complained that life at work was dull and all she wanted to do was get out into the fresh air and feel the exhilaration of being 20,000 feet up a craggy mountain. She had created two completely contrasting pictures in her mind. Climbing was exciting, vibrant, multi-coloured, a huge panorama and a sense of being totally alive. Work was dreary, languid, grey and static. No wonder she wasn't enjoying it! We played around with the work representation and took some of the pictures and feelings from climbing and put them into the work place. She noticed that it changed her response to work and gave her a fresh approach to her job, in addition to her retaining great pictures of herself in the mountains.

Some people tend to keep their negative experiences at the forefront of their mind and can become bogged down in the challenges they continually seem to face. Others keep their big, bright, positive experiences in the foreground, so their resourcefulness is accessed first and enables them to approach challenges with more confidence and expectations of a great result.

Next time you are thinking about a painful or unpleasant memory, make the picture dark, small and away from you. Change the voices to comic ones, for example, Bugs Bunny, and change the music to honky tonk. Then notice the difference. Change your self-talk too. When you say 'I am stressed', that is an identity statement. If you change that to 'I feel stressed', you have moved to the behavioural level and change is much easier.

'Two men looked out through the prison bars. One saw mud, the other the stars.' Dale Carnegie

Which way do you look when you are getting stressed? When you focus on the mud, you can get stuck and bogged down, when you look up to the stars you feel hope and energy.

Satir's categories

The way you will respond to stress varies depending on your personality, early upbringing and life experiences. Everyone has their own pattern of warning signs and stress responses. If you know yours, you can gauge the depth of a problem by the intensity of your symptoms and changes in your behaviour. As you become better acquainted with your team, you will be able to recognise their stress responses and be able to help defuse them more quickly. There are many behavioural symptoms to be aware of and here a few:

Feeling:
- Upset, worried, tearful.
- Irritated by others.
- Out of control.
- A failure.
- Demotivated.
- Misunderstood.
- Powerless.

Difficulty with:
- Sleeping.
- Concentration.

Making decisions
Loss of:
- Creativity.
- Interest in appearance.
- Interest in others.

You can also experience a loss or increase to your appetites – eating, drinking, smoking and sex. A good indicator of the presence of debilitating stress is the intensification of personality traits, so that a person who is careful becomes over-fussy, a person who is anxious becomes panic-stricken, someone who is insecure becomes vulnerable and someone who is irritable becomes volatile. There are also physical symptoms such as stomach and digestive disorders, skin problems, headaches and backaches.

Just take a minute to think about yourself and your team members. What stress responses come into play when any of you are under pressure and feeling unresourceful? As you consider it now, perhaps you can realise that any extreme behaviours you have experienced can be explained as a stress response and if so they can be handled in a different way. Rather than branding someone's behaviour as deliberately difficult, perhaps you can attempt to work out what might have pushed them into stress, and what you can do to help them.

In one of her seminal books, *Peoplemaking* (1990), Virginia Satir suggested that whenever stress occurred there were four unsupportive response patterns that would habitually follow. These four patterns would be evident when the stressed person felt their self-esteem was diminished, resulting in them doubting their self worth. These she labelled:

- the Placater.
- the Blamer.
- the Computer.
- the Distracter.

She argued that when your self esteem is high, there is a fifth pattern. Stress may be painful or annoying but it doesn't threaten your core being. The label for a person reacting in this way is the Leveller.

The Placater

The placater is frightened that other people will become angry, go away and never come back again. Their aim is to get people to be nice to them and so they back down and go with whatever other people want. They typically ask forgiveness and say: 'Whatever anybody else wants is fine by me' or 'Sorry'.

The Blamer

The blamer uses verbal patterns intended to demonstrate that they are in charge, the boss, the one with power. They shift responsibility to others. They shout first, so others won't shout at them. They can sulk, or hit out. They may even say nothing, hide it and then launch a surprise attack when everyone thinks the worst is over. They typically say: 'It's your fault.'

The Computer or Super Reasonable

This type of person is terrified that someone will find out what their feelings are, so they make out that they don't have any. They commonly dissociate and avoid saying 'I' and may use 'one' or 'you' instead. They typically say: 'It is obvious that there is no problem here.' 'No rational person would be alarmed by this.'

The Distracter

Distracters continually switch from one category to another due to an underlying feeling of panic. They do whatever they can to deflect attention and shift the focus. They typically say: 'It wasn't me.'

The Leveller

The leveller genuinely 'levels' with you and what they say is what they feel. The leveller gives frank information. Their response represents the truth of the person at a moment of time. The response is congruent, so the words, tone and body convey the same message. They typically say; 'We need to work out what is happening here.' 'This is how it seems to me.'

Susan Quilliam offers some great ideas for being the Leveller and managing people in your team who are not.

'A placater is chiefly scared of your disapproval, so give reassurance. Find some way to tell them they're fine, an "ideal client", "brilliant colleague". They'll soon chill out and be more able to think clearly.

A blamer has a deep fear of being blamed themselves – so blaming in return will only stoke the flames. And steer them away from blaming comments about third parties – instead, get them defining what exactly the problem is and what can be done about it.

A computer will simply freeze and stop thinking. Once they've chilled out, however, their brains will click into gear and you can get them running the same mental approach that works with a blamer. Ask factual questions, make practical suggestions, create an action plan "get a solution".

A distracter will try to divert your attention. So don't fall for long explanations, excuses or reasons "why" the crisis arose. Instead, ask direct, "closed" questions ones to which the answers are "yes" or "no" in order to get clear what is happening and move things on.'

(Extract from *What Makes People Tick? The ultimate guide to personality types* by Susan Quilliam.)

Detachment – a way to reduce your stress

A sense of detachment is an excellent way of combating external stress or dealing with destructive emotions. The two following techniques will help you to stop and rethink how you might react to a potentially stressful situation and how to take care of your well being.

The first is regularly to repeat the following phrases which will detach you from destructive emotions or feelings. They are very simple and very empowering:

- I have behaviours and I am more than those behaviours.
- I have feelings and I am more than those feelings.
- I have thoughts and I am more than those thoughts.
- I am greater than those behaviours, feelings and thoughts.
- I control them; they do not control me.

I heard a lovely variation on this at a meditation event recently. It was: 'I am the thinker, not the thoughts.'

The second detachment technique can be practised as a visualisation. It is called the bell jar technique. Imagine you have an inverted, perspex bell jar surrounding you. This container acts as a barrier and stops other people's negative thoughts and feelings from reaching or touching you.

Let the past go and forgive. Dragging parts of your past with you only slows you down. If you stay hurt, depressed, angry, frustrated or humiliated, to name but five options, you impact on yourself much more significantly than on anyone else. Others may notice that you're antisocial or crabby from time to time but the bad feelings are with you all the time. And who does not forgiving really hurt? Forgiving others – or yourself – does not mean forgetting or condoning what happened. When you forgive, you move on. When you don't, you are rooted to the same spot or even move backwards in your own despair. It is your choice and your emotional health that are affected. To release the shackles of the past, you must be willing to forgive.

Conclusion

You and your team will feel great benefits when any of the tips below become integrated into your routine as habitual behaviours. Pick a new one each week and enjoy being able to think more clearly and work more effectively.

1. Make time to relax!
To relax you need to give yourself permission, to grant yourself a little time in which to practise. It sure beats having a heart attack! It also beats anxiety and exhaustion. Don't waste your precious life on feeling exhausted. Fifteen minutes a day of relaxation practice makes a huge difference.

2. When you finish for the day, take 15 minutes for yourself
Agree with the family that you all need time to leave work / school behind you to get into enjoying time together. Your work, of course, may be based in your home. You could also agree a 15-minute period to offload together and then get on with enjoying your evening. If you keep mulling things over that have affected you during the day, you are letting them negatively influence your evening.

3. Try open-eyed meditation
One way of doing this is by gazing softly, not staring, at a candle flame. Darken the room, light a candle, sit comfortably and gaze at the flame. The aim is to have a focus for the mind. So when your mind wanders, gently bring your attention back to the flame. Calming the mind is the basis of all relaxation techniques: that is why you will feel warm and relaxed after doing the exercise.

4. Take aerobic exercise

When you are stressed, cortisol builds up in your body and makes you feel stressed. The more stressed you are, the more cortisol (the 'stress hormone') your body makes and the more stressed you feel. Have physical fun. Do things with your body. Aerobic exercise flushes it out of your system. All you need is 15 minutes. This will help you to think more clearly and plan your time more effectively. Take up dancing, tai chi, yoga, Pilates, running or walking, with a friend if possible.

5. Laugh and smile

Smiling makes you feel better and helps you to think in a more positive way. This in turn helps you to see more possible solutions to your problems. Frowning reduces the options you are able to see. Watch your favourite comedy programmes, listen to your favourite comedies, read books and poems that make you laugh or devise and draw cartoons of situations that might otherwise stress you.

6. Read, sing or dance

Immerse yourself in a book or magazine you've been meaning to read. Put on your favourite music to sing along with or dance to. If you have mediation / relaxation music, that can also help. Relaxation can be uptime or downtime.

7. Learn to relax

Listen to a relaxation tape, follow a relaxation DVD and switch off from everything else to think about your body and mind. Practise deep breathing and create affirmations to repeat regularly: 'I can relax in all situations.' 'I am calm and able to handle whatever comes my way.' 'I am free to be me.' Put these into your screen saver or welcome note on your mobile phone. Paste them around your home to remind yourself to relax. meditate regularly.

8. Pamper yourself

Take a bubble bath or a long, hot shower. Listen to music that you enjoy. Light a scented candle. Start the bath running. Add aromatherapy bath salts or bubble bath and breathe deeply of the fragrant steam. Give your skin whatever treatments you like, and finish up with a soothing face mask. Turn off the water and step into the bath. Lie down. Sigh! Close your eyes and let your thoughts drift. It's almost impossible to worry while lying in hot water, breathing in fragrant steam, with candle light dancing all around and soft music playing.

9. Prepare for a good night's sleep

Do you toss and turn in bed worrying about the day that's gone and the one that follows? Set aside five minutes before going to bed and write down, record or some way collect all your concerns. Then put them aside until tomorrow and forget about them. You don't need to spend your sleep time with them, you know you won't forget them. The chances are they will have lessened greatly after a good night's sleep. You can leave them in the good care of your unconscious to sort through while you're sleeping. Think about all the good things in your life, instead of the 'not so good'. You may even catch yourself smiling before you go to sleep.

Finale

'You said we're a team. One person struggles, we all struggle. One person triumphs, we all triumph.' from the film, Coach Carter

'If you want to be a great leader – you have to learn to be a follower.' Coach Carter

The best ideas come from your people – and your role is to create the conditions to tap into this talent and foster contribution. This requires you to give up control – and to trust your team to do the right thing, with appropriate coaching, development and support from you. How often do you encourage others in the team to run team meetings. Stop feeling you have to have all the answers and routinely ask team members: what could we improve and really listen to their suggestions?

One final thought

'The announcement came as an item in the news only recently. Scientists had just discovered what might be the ultimate self-help cure for cancer. At a research laboratory they had taken seratonin, which is the hormone produced by the brain when we are happy, placed it in a test tube of cancer cells, and it had instantly killed every cell. Asked why it had taken so long to make this discovery, their reply was simple. "There are a million chemicals which could be tested on cancer and we have only just got round to trying seratonin." So there you are, scientific proof that happiness heals. It may be a new truth to the world of science, but it is not new to many who have intuitively known for a very long time.'

Mike George, The 7 Ahas of Highly Enlightened Souls

INSTANT TIP

Learn to recognise your stress signals and your team's, and act to reduce them.

Glossary

Activist   Learning style where the learner's preference is to involve themselves fully and likes activity.

Anchors   Any stimulus that evokes a consistent response.

Associated   Seeing, hearing and feeling, as if you are inside an experience.

Auditory   The sense of sound which relates to hearing and speaking in the neuro of NLP.

Behavioural flexibility   Openness to changing behaviour to meet preferred outcomes.

Beliefs   Determine the way we behave and shape our decision-making processes.

Blamer   Satir category who responds to stress by blaming others through a deep fear of being blamed themselves.

Calibration   Using rapport skills to recognise and interpret different information that is unique to each person.

Computer   Satir category who responds to stress with over-reasoned argument through terror that someone will find out what their feelings are.

Conscious mind   What is in your present awareness.

Dissociated   Watching yourself from the outside of an experience.

Distracter   Satir category who will try to divert your attention.

Eye accessing cues   Eye movements which indicate visual, auditory or kinaesthetic thinking.

Frame   How you contextualise what is going on around you and set a frame round it.

Kinaesthetic   The sense of feeling, experiencing and touch in the neuro of NLP.

Leveller   Satir category who responds to stress 'on the level' and who wants to work out causes and solutions.

Meta model   Identifies ambiguities and targets them with questions.

Metaphor   Create a state of inventiveness, openness and acceptance through story and comparison.

Metaprograms   The unconscious filters we use to sort the information we receive in a systematic way which then determines our behaviours.

Milton model   'Artfully vague' language that is deliberately ambiguous and abstract.

Modelling   Observing and recreating someone else's successful behaviours or attitudes.

Operating principles   Assumptions that form the basis of NLP thinking. Also called *presuppositions*.

Outcome   Sensory-based goal or desired state.

Perceptual positions   Analysing a situation from three perspectives: yours, theirs and from a neutral position.

Placater   Satir category who responds to stress by asking forgiveness and is scared of your disapproval.

Pragmatist   Learning style where the learner's preference is to be practical and get straight to the point.

Predicates   The words we use that differentiate between the representational systems.

Rapport   The process of building and sustaining a relationship of mutual trust, harmony and understanding.

Reflector   Learning style where the learner's preference is to collect all the facts before embarking on a project.

Representational systems   Internal coding based on the five senses: seeing, hearing, touching, smelling and tasting.

Satir categories   four unsupportive response patterns to stress (placater, blamer, computer and distracter) and one supportive response (leveller).

State   All the thoughts, emotions, and physiology that you express in any given moment.

Submodalities   How we code experiences and distinguish different sensory systems.

Theorist   Learning style where the learner's preference is to approach situations logically and work through step by step.

Unconscious mind   Where your memories, beliefs, identities and your past experiences are stored.

Visual   The sense of sight in the neuro of NLP.

Well formedness   Structure to ensure outcomes are compelling and demonstrable.

References

Bandler, R. (1977) *Using your Brain for a Change*, Boulder, CO: Real People Press.

Bandler, R. and Grinder, J. (1985) *Frogs into Princes*, Boulder, CO: Real People Press.

Bavister, S. and Vickers, A. (2004) *Teach Yourself NLP*, London: Hodder Education.

Bradbury, A. (2006) *Develop Your NLP Skills*, 3rd edn, London: Kogan Page.

Covey, Stephen R. (1999) *The Seven Habits of Highly Effective People*, London: Simon & Schuster.

George, M. (2003) *The 7 Ahas of Highly Enlightened Souls*, Oakland, CA: O Books.

Hazeldine, S. (2005) *Bare Knuckle Selling*, Great Yarmouth: Lean Marketing Press.

Honey, P. and Mumford, A. (1982) *Manual of Learning Styles*, Maidenhead: Peter Honey Publications.

Jackson, P. Z. and McKergow, M. (2006) *The Solutions Focus: Making Coaching and Change SIMPLE*, 2nd edn, London: Nicholas Brealey Publishing.

Knight, S. (2002) *NLP at Work*, London: Nicholas Brealey Publishing.

Lickorish, S. (2003) 'Storytelling: How to Enrich the Learning Experience', *Train the Trainer*, Ely: Fenman Ltd.

McClelland, F (2006) *How to Influence With Your Voice*, Vocaltrademark.com.

McConnon, S. and McConnon, M. (2004) *Resolving Conflict: How to Manage Disagreements and Develop Trust and Understanding*, Oxford: How to Books.

McDermott, I. and Jago, W. (2001) *The NLP Coach*, London: Piatkus Books.

McDermott, I. and O'Connor, J. (1997) *Practical NLP for Managers*, Aldershot: Gower Publishing.

Mereu, F.G. (2007) *Acceder à vos Ressources*, St Julien-en-Genevois: Editions Jouvence.

Mitchell, W. (1997) *It's Not What Happens To You, It's What You Do About It*, Arvada, CO: W. Mitchell.

Molden, D. (2001) *NLP Business Masterclass*, London: Financial Times Prentice Hall.

O'Connor, J. and Seymour, J. (1997) *Introducing NLP*, 2nd edn, London: Thorsons.

Overdurf, J. and Silverthorn, J. (2000) *NLP Practitioner Field Manual and Study Guide*, Scottsdale, AZ: Neuro-Energetics.

Overdurf, J. and Silverthorn, J. (1995) *Training Trances*, Portland, OR: Metamorphous Press.

Plaice, T. (2006) *Face the Music and Win: How to Follow Your Passion and Conquer Your Fear*, Leics: Brave Press.

Quilliam, S. (2003) *What Makes People Tick?*, London: HarperCollins.

Robbins, A. (1977) *Unlimited Power*, London: Simon & Schuster.

Satir, V. (1990) *Peoplemaking*, London: Condor Books.

Shapiro, M. (2001) *Shift Your Thinking, Change Your Life*, London: Sheldon Press.

Silva, J and Goldman, B. (1990) *The Silva Mind Control Method of Mental Dynamics*, London: Pocket Books.

Smart, J. Grafton (2006) *NLP Coaching Cards*, Leicester: Wordsalad Publications

Contacts

Alison Smith – landscapingyourlife.co.uk
Andrew Whittaker – peopledevelopmentworks.com
Chris Davidson – activepresence.co.uk
Fergus McClelland – socialtrademark.com
Francesca Giulia Mereu – waterlogic.li
Jamie Smart – saladltd.co.uk
John Overdurf and Julie Silverthorn – Neuro-energetics – nlptrainings.com
Maria Deacon-Viney – remarkablesuccess.co.uk
Marie Mosely.com – mariemosely.com
Mo Shapiro – moshapiro.com
Shay McConnon – shaymcconnon.com
Simon Hazeldine – simonhazeldine.com
Stephanie Holland and David Morton – rapport-online.com
Susan Quilliam – susanquilliam.com
Tracy Plaice – tracyplaice.com

Index